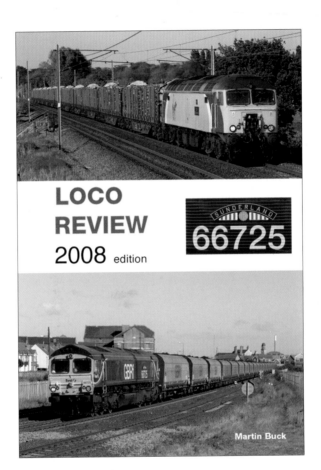

LOCO REVIEW

SUNDERLAND
66725

2008 edition

Martin Buck

FREIGHTMASTER

PUBLISHING

CONTENTS

Published by :

Freightmaster Publishing
158 Overbrook
SWINDON
SN3 6AY

01793 - 644957

www.freightmasterpublishing.co.uk

First published : December 2007

ISBN : 0-9537540-8-1

Printed By :

Stephens & George
Goat Mill Road
Dowlais
MERTHYR TYDFIL
CF48 3TD

Cover Design : Martin Buck

PREFACE

Loco Review - the 2008 edition - is a collection of excellent images, many submitted by well known photographers, depicting the locomotives which helped to make 2007 such a fascinating year. There have also been several interesting new freight flows, plus the introduction of new rolling stock, which are also featured.

The book builds on the previous 'Loco Hauled 2006' and 'Railfreight 2005' yearbooks, but this time with a new title and a change of emphasis. As well as the regular features, there are an extra 48 pages (with no retail price increase, I might add!) and three new sections:

Special Events : A look at the 'Twenty 20s Gala' at Barrow Hill, DRS Carlisle Kingmoor open day and Class 66/7 namings.

Anniversaries : A tribute to four diesel Classes celebrating an anniversary in 2007.

Guest photographer Hugh Ballantyne dips into his archive for a selection of Deltics, Westerns, Class 20s and Class 31s at work in their hey-day during the BR Blue era.

Heritage : Here, a look at what's been going on at a selection of preserved lines around the country and the sheer variety of 'Classic' diesel traction on offer - something that enthusiasts flock to see.

Highlights readily spring to mind ....
- First GBRf coal trains
- Virgin Class 57/3s on timber traffic
- 'Barbie' liveried Class 66/7s
- Colas Rail and DRS 57s on RHTTs

.... not to mention the return to mainline running of Deltic 'Royal Scots Grey', D1015's run to Aberystwyth and the spectacle of No 40145 in large-Logo livery!

Many thanks go to all the people who have kindly contributed images - I have been simply inundated - without which it would have been impossible to compile this publication. A list of contributors and associated websites can be found on page 144.

Remember the 2009 edition starts here, so get those cameras out and send in your images. If you need a reminder of how interesting the rail scene is, please flick through the following pages and enjoy!

Martin Buck

TIMBER

Thunderbirds are go!

January 2007 sees a new Company enter the UK railfreight market - Amec Spie Rail - having been awarded a five-year contract to transport timber to Chirk for Kronsopan from loading points in Scotland and Carlisle Yard. Kronsopan, being a long-term user of rail, is one of the world's largest producers of wood products, which includes chipboard and fibreboard, requiring nearly 250,000 tonnes of timber each year to satisfy its demand.

The Company is hiring three Class 57/3s from Virgin Trains and conveying the timber in converted IGA steel carriers and converted KFA Cargowaggons. Consequently, this spells the end of the 2-axle OTA open timber wagons, which have been a familiar sight on the WCML for many years.

The IGA bogie flat wagons will be used for the first few months until receiving 12 KFA timber carriers, converted by WH Davis, Langwith Junction, from former GE Rail Services vans. These KFAs are allocated to operating pool 0866.

The service is initially running three days a week from Carlisle with plans to run daily when traffic resumes from Crianlarich.

6Z57,	13:29 Carlisle Yard - Chirk	FSX
6Z58,	23:07 Chirk - Carlisle Yard	FSX

The loaded train runs via Chester; the returning empties via Shrewsbury and Crewe.

(Above) : According to the old station clock, Class 57/3 No 57308 'Tin Tin' passes Carnforth 10-minutes early of the 'booked' time of 15:50hrs on 30th May with 6Z57, the 13:29 Carlisle Yard - Chirk.   (John Rudd)

Overleaf

(Page 4) : On 3rd May, No 57304 'Gordon Tracy' passes Red Bank, Newton Le Willows, with 6Z57, Carlisle -Chirk loaded timber service formed of a rake of the smarter looking KFA wagons.   (Anthony Allen)

(Page 5): First day of trials, 24th January .... No 57301 'Scott Tracy' reverses the loaded IGA wagons past the drum dryer into the Kronospan sidings at Chirk - how neatly would the 57 fit into that dryer? Chirk is located on the Wrexham - Shrewsbury main line, close to the Anglo-Welsh border.   (Richard Jones)

FREIGHT FLOWS

CONSTRUCTION MATERIALS

EWS - HOAs Take Hold

Following a brief trial using HGA 'Gunnells' on a new Anglo-Scottish sand flow from Middleton Towers to Mossend, EWS dispense with these old wagons and replace them with their own HOA bogie hopper wagons, complete with *EWS Construction* branding. The HGAs will gradually be phased out on other routes as HOAs take hold across the network.

Initilal flows utilising the new HOAs are:

6S88,	Middleton Towers - Ayr Harbour	TThO
6A21,	East Usk - Hayes	TThSO
6E17,	Peak Forest - Leeds	ThX

(Above) : The new EWS branding for their Construction division.

(Opposite) : EWS-liveried Class 60 No 60018 has arrived at Peak Forest with the 6M17 empties from Leeds Stourton on 2nd May formed entirely of the new EWS HOA bogie hoppers.

(Below) : A reminder of the 'old order'.... No 60055 'Thomas Barnardo' approaches Swindon station on 1st March with a rake of HGA 'Gunnells', running as 6C23, Hayes - East Usk stone empties. (All Martin Buck)

FREIGHT FLOWS

(Above) : No 60068 'Charles Darwin' passes Normanton on Soar, 6th July, hauling 6M87, Ely Papworth - Peak Forest empty HOA bogie hoppers, the first five of which are in the new 'Cemex' colours.   (Paul Biggs)

(Below) : New traction, new flow for the displaced ex-RMC JGAs. Class 66/0 No 66197 heads along the 'Up' relief on the Great Western Main Line at Iver on 24th July with 6Z20, the 09:45 Whatley - St. Pancras loaded stone hoppers - note, the JGAs have had their RMC branding 'blacked out'.   (Martin Blois)

FREEGHT FLOWS

COAL

FIRST GBRf

Breaking new ground .... by far the most important development for GBRf in 2007 is the company's decision to move into a completely new railfreight market - coal!

After a number of trials testing out their own purpose-built HYA bogie coal hoppers, GBRf begin working a new flow of imported coal from Tyne Dock to Drax Power Station on 2nd April. The new high-capacity HYA bogie hoppers were built at the Astra Vagoane Works in Arad, Romania, which is owned by International Railway Systems, and incorporate Axiom Rail TF25 low trackforce bogies. Apparently, these hoppers are not going to be painted above Solebar height, resulting in a weight saving of 200kg per wagon, which will effectively mean that more coal can be carried.

The full train plan for this new flow is as follows:

6H93,	06:51	Tyne Dock - Drax	MWFO
4N92,	13:45	Drax - Tyne Dock	MWFO
6H90,	11:26	Tyne Dock - Drax	TThO
4N93,	19:13	Drax - Tyne Dock	TThO
6H92,	19:23	Tyne Dock - Drax	MWFO
4N90,	01:15	Drax - Tyne Dock	MWFO

The first diagram is routed via the Durham Coast in both directions and the other two diagrams are routed via the East Coast Main Line. First GB Railfreight also sign a contract to move a further 800,000 tonnes of imported coal annually from Hull Docks to EDF power stations at Cottam and West Burton but, due to the high cost of imported Russian coal, these flows are put on hold and coal is sourced from local mines as an alternative, thus:

6B22,	08:00	Welbeck Colliery - West Burton
4G23,	12:34	West Burton - Thoresby
6B23,	10:00	Thoresby - West Burton

Previous page:

On 9th August, Metronet-liveried No. 66719 'Metro-Land' passes through the small station halt of Knottingley with 6H93, the 06:51 Tyne Dock - Drax loaded coal hoppers. (Martin Buck)

(Top Right) : In readiness for the new coal flows, various positioning moves occur to get the imported HYA coal hoppers into place to start operations. On 27th March, the second HYA move takes place and Class 66/7 No 66711 enters Camden Road station with 4Z66, the 14:30 Wembley - York Holgate. (Nigel Gibbs)

(Bottom Right) : On 1st July, Class 87s No 87022 'Cock o the North' + No 87028 'Lord President' haul 4Z77, the 10:34 Willesden - Doncaster along the ECML at Retford with 22 new HYAs in tow. This train may, perhaps, qualify for 'Working of the Year', especially as the Class 87s are destined for Bulgaria later in the year! (Mick Tindall)

Page 12:

The Durham coastline is a dramatic setting for No. 66721 'Harry Beck' as it sweeps round the curves at Hawthorn Dene on 10th July with 6H90, the 11:33 Tyne Dock - Drax power station. (Karl Sherman)

Page 13 :

With overhead power lines dominating the view, No. 66709 'Joseph Arnold Davies' approaches Knottingley with 4N92, the 13:45 Drax - Tyne Dock coal empties on 10th July. (David Stracey)

FHH

As a general rule, apart from GBRf's move into the coal sector, power station coal trains rarely make the headlines, but Freightliner *Heavy Haul* start running three new services which are certainly newsworthy.

1. Hatfield Mine

This new service is significant for two reasons - it is the first coal traffic to leave Hatfield for three years, and it means that Freightliner is now operating coal trains into Ratcliffe power station, previously an EWS stronghold. Two trains a week are running out of the mine:

6Z85, 11:18 Hatfield Mine - Ratcliffe   TThO

(Above) : This is the typical view from the station footbridge at Hatfield & Stainforth looking towards the Mine. Luck is on the photographers side on 30th August - sun and trains - combining for a rare triple shot. In the background is Hatfield colliery and No 66952 waiting to depart with 6Z85 to Ratcliffe, while No 66617 applies the brakes as it enters Stainforth station with 6R10, Immingham - Barrow Hill loaded coal hoppers and No 60041 powers towards Doncaster with 6D75, Scunthorpe - Doncaster Belmont rails. (Alan Hazelden)

(Opposite) : No 66513 draws forward with 4Z85, Wintersett - Hatfield on the first day of operations (24th July) and the first wagon is loaded with coal from the newly reopened seams of Hatfield Main Colliery. After loading, the train will form 6Z85, the 11:18 departure for Ratcliffe power station. (Rob Terrace)

2. Greenburn to Ratcliffe

This is a direct 'cherry pick' from EWS - it even uses the same headcode and departure time:

> 6M32, 09:37 Greenburn - Ratcliffe p.s. SX

However, unlike the EWS version, it is routed via the Settle & Carlisle, rather than the WCML, and after discharging at Ratcliffe, the empties run to Immingham, to form a loaded train to Drax, from where they run back to Greenburn:

> 4S73, 18:37 Drax p.s. - Greenburn SX

3. Portbury to Rugeley

The third new service is the first FHH coal train to run from Portbury, initially running as an 'out and back' service, but now that EWS are once again using the 6V17 path to Portbury, the train is amended to run as follows:

> 4Z84, 21:30 Rugeley p.s. - Portbury   SX   (off 6M51 from Hull)
> 6Z82, 07:00 Portbury - Rugeley p.s.   SX
> 4Z83, 15:30 Rugeley p.s. - Leeds Hunslet SX

To avoid the need for a banking engine, 6Z82 is routed via Severn Tunnel, Abergavenny, Hereford and Telford - this also removes the need to run round anywhere en route!

FREIGHT FLOWS

(Above) : The inaugural run .... *FHH* start running coal trains from Portbury Docks to Rugeley power station from 9th July, although *FHH* have previously worked out of Portbury Docks running 6X42, Portbury - Mossend car train. No 66564 approaches Dorrington in less than favourable photographic conditions with 6Z28, the 07.00 Portbury Docks - Rugeley Power Station coal train, sporting a 'Bristol Herons On Tour' headboard. (Richard Jones)

(Below) : On 2 August, No 66518 passes the site of the old goods yard at Pill on the Portishead Branch line with 6Z82, early into its journey hauling 19 loaded HXA wagons. A section of the elevated M5 motorway, which spans both the railway line and the River Avon, can be seen in the background. (Richard Giles)

EWS

'MEAs' to Scotland

A new service commences in August, initially running once a week, conveying coal from New Cumnock loading point in Scotland to Ketton cement works:

> 6Z89, 02:32 Healey Mills - New Cumnock   THO   Q
>
> 6M16, 17:41 New Cumnock - Ketton   THO   Q

The empties run via the Settle & Carlisle overnight and recess in Carlisle yard, from where they take the path of 6S13, Warrington - New Cumnock empty HTAs. The loaded train runs via Hexham, York, Chesterfield and Melton Mowbray.

Most interestingly, this new flow takes MEAs to Scotland for the first time in many years!

'MBAs' to Rugby

Many cement works around the country do not have automatic discharge facilities and the coal is normally delivered in 2-axle MEA box wagons, to:

> Clitheroe   Ketton   Penyffordd   Rugby

However, the supply to the Cemex cement works at Rugby is now being conveyed in 'Monster' MBA wagons, released off the finished Northwich - Drax flyash flow, although the workings remain unaltered:

> 6M86, 20:48 Immingham - Rugby   TThO
>
> 6E11, 09:30 Rugby - Immingham   FO

(Above) : EWS Class 66/0 No 66148 approaches East Holmes signalbox, quarter of a mile to the west of Lincoln station, on 6th September with 6E11, Rugby - Immingahm empty MBAs. Under the Lincoln track and resignalling modernisation programme, East Holmes signalbox is scheduled for removal in August 2008.   (Nic Joynson)

FREIGHT FLOWS

CONSTRUCTION MATERIALS
FHH

Not to be outdone, Freightliner Heavy Haul introduce some new stone hoppers into traffic and move existing wagons onto different flows. For example:

New HIA hoppers :

6M42, Wool - Neasden

6M17, Croft - Neasden

6Z23, Burngullow - Hackney Yard

JGAs :

6A28, Cardiff Pengam - Thorney MIll

6O58, Cardiff Pengam - Angerstein

(Above) : PGA - No. VTG14213   Wool Sand Terminal

(Below) : PGA - No. VTG14348   Swindon

The HIAs ostensibly replace PGAs in the number range VTG14203 - 14461, whilst the JGAs replace the incumbent PGAs (number range VTG 14346 - 14385), which return to the leasing company, pending new work from EWS later in the year. A photograph of these displaced wagons is included to complete the picture.

(Opposite) : Deep in the heart of the former Southern Region on 15th March, No 66507 makes for an interesting composition as it passes Addlestone Moor, Chertsey, with 6O49, Wool - Neasden empty sand hoppers; the train consisting entirely of the new HIA bogie hoppers.   (David Stracey)

(Below) : A rake of JGAs make up the consist of 6B11, Thorney Mill - Cardiff Pengam empty stone hoppers seen passing Denchworth on the Great Western Mainline on 4th September, hauled by Class 66/5 No 66560. These JGAs have been christened 'Jolly Green Giants' by rail enthusiasts!   (Martin Buck - 3)

(Above) : On Tuesday, 17th April, No 66582 passes Aller Junction hauling 6Z22, the 15:25 Moorswater – Earles sidings empty cement tanks; the first time this train runs since 24th August 2006 - a most welcome addition to the south west of England freight scene.

(Below) : Meanwhile, on 1st May, No 66552 hauls 6M37, Moorswater – Earles Sidings empty cement tanks past the well-known location of Cockwood Harbour with a rake of PCAs, inclusive of both straight and depressed centre barrel designs. (Both Robert Sherwood)

CEMENT

Moorswater Resurrection

After a seven month absence, the Lafarge Blue Circle cement flow between Earles Sidings and Moorswater resumes running in April, two / three times a week, using PCA 2-axle tank wagons. The service is:

6V20, 18:36 Earles Sidings - Moorswater		Q
6M37, 15:25 Moorswater - Earles Sidings		Q

INFRASTRUCTURE

Sleepers

Following the opening of the infrastucture Fairwater Yard at Taunton in late 2006, First GB Railfreight (GBRf) win the contract to move concrete sleepers in conjuntion with the renewal of the West of England main line. New sleepers are moved overnight from Peterborough whilst the old ones are transported during daylight hours, affording photographers the opportunity to record this service for the archive. The flow is:

4V11, 18:45 Peterborough - Taunton Fairwater	TThFO	
4E31, 06:34 Fairwater Yard - Peterborough	TThFO	

Rails

Due to the cessation of rail production at Workington, Scunthorpe is now taking over the mantle with several trains of rails leaving the steelworks:

GBRf	4M20, 09:25 Scunthorpe - Wellingborough	TO	Q
	4E10, 15:24 Wellingborough - Scunthorpe	MO	Q
EWS	6M02, 15:30 Scunthorpe - Crewe		
	6E02, 10:09 Crewe - Scunthorpe		
	6D75, 09:17 Scunthorpe - Doncaster Belmont		Q
	6D74, 06:54 Doncaster Belmont - Scunthorpe		Q

In addition, the following loaded service can run, if required:

6X78, 17:16 Scunthorpe - Doncaster Belmont

Interestingly, due to production of rails at Scunthorpe steelworks not reaching full capacity, rails are being imported into Workington Docks, resulting in the following new flow:

6X43, 15:45 Workington - Eastleigh	MThO	Q
4M28, 221:06 Eastleigh - Carlisle Yard	MWO	Q

MINERALS

GBRf Gain East Leake Gypsum

GBRf secure a new flow of gypsum from West Burton Power Station to the British Gypsum plant at Hotchley Hill, East Leake, which is situated 5-miles from Loughborough South Junction on the now single line track of the ex-Great Central Railway running to the Nottingham Heritage Centre:

4M80, 20:02 West Burton - Hotchley Hill	Q	Loaded	
4E80, 13:11 Hotchley Hill - West Burton	Q	Empties	

FREIGHT FLOWS

(Above) : On a glorious summer day, No 66703 'Doncaster PSB 1981 - 2002' passes Styles Hill on 28th June with 4E31, Fairwater Yard - Peterborough. (Nic Joynson)

(Below) : 'Medite'liveried No 66709 'Joseph Arnold Davies' is seen on the ex-Great Central Line crossing the River Soar Viaduct at Stanford on 19th April with a rake of empty gypsum containers. (Paul Biggs)

(Above) : No 66724 passes Kilnhurst (Swinton) on 4th September with a colourful train formation conveying rails for the 'Metronet' project, running as 4M20, Scunthorpe - Wellingborough. (Andy Small)

(Below) : On 9th August, 6E02 Crewe - Scunthorpe empty rails is worked by a pair of EWS 37s, No. 37422 'Cardiff Canton' + No 37410, seen passing through Horbury Cutting, just to the east of Healey Mills. (John Rudd)

(Above) : With the Port of Tees Dock providing the backdrop, No 66607 leads 6F23, Tees Dock - Boulby potash empties on 23rd August along the single track and out of the docks area to Grangetown 'Down' goods loop, where the locomotive will run-round before proceeding to Boulby.

(Top Right) : This composition shows Class 66/6 No 66609 slowly pulling out of Middlesbrough Goods Yard on 18th April with empty JGAs forming 6F35, Middlesbrough - Boulby. Upon joining the main line at Newport East Junction, the locomotive will have to run round its train in order to head for the Boulby branch.   (Anthony Allen)

(Below) : The exterior of Grangetown signalbox must rank as one of the grimiest of all 'boxes on the rail network. It stands adjacent to the 'Down' goods line and is where No 66531 is seen (after running round) preparing to set off on the final leg of the journey with 6F32, Boulby - Tees Dock loaded potash hoppers.   (Both Martin Buck)

MINERALS

Boulby Goes Green

Freightliner Heavy Haul secure a five year contract to move more than 1.5 million tonnes of minerals on behalf of Cleveland Potash. The flows are Potash and Rock Salt from the Company's mine at Boulby on the Yorkshire coast, which is one of the deepest underground mines in Europe, situated at the end of a 12-mile long single line from Saltburn. The Potash goes to Tees Dock for use as fertilizer and a compound in both the glass-making and pharmaceutical industries, while the Rock Salt goes to the Cobra terminal, Middlesbrough, stockpiled for road treatment use.

METROLINK

Get Shorty!

A major program of track renewal on the Manchester to Bury section of the Metrolink network is being undertaken by Carillion this summer and EWS win the contract to supply ballast to a stockpile at Bury, running via the Heywood branch of the East Lancs Railway. Ballast trains will comprise 3 sets of upto 40 MEAs and one set of 20 MCA / MDA / MOAs.

However, the stars of the show are three reduced height Class 08 shunters (Nos 08993 / 08994 and 08995) which EWS have had overhauled and repainted in their corporate livery at Doncaster to act as works train locomotives, due to restricted overhead clearances on the Metrolink system. One may recall these 08s found fame in the 1980s, when they replaced Class 03s on the gauge restricted Burry Port & Gwendraeth Valley line from Kidwelly to Cwmmawr, until workings ceased in 1996.

(Overleaf) : On 28th August, this superbly lit image depicts two of the three restricted height Class 08s (Nos 08994 and 08995), complete with Carillion logo stickers on the bodyside, stabled outside the shed at Buckley Wells on the East Lancashire Railway. (Fred Kerr)

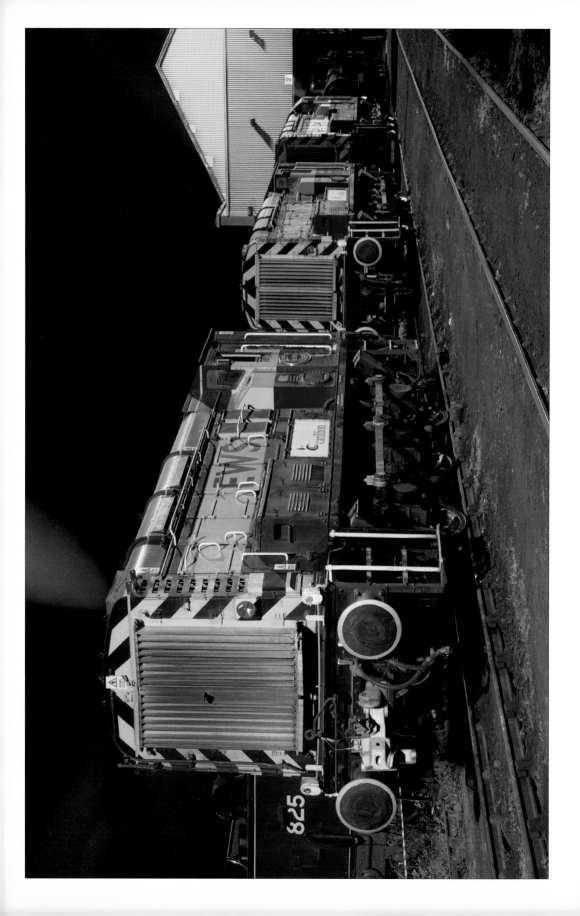

FREIGHT FLOWS

RAILHEAD TREATMENT TRAINS

Enter Colas Rail ....

Colas Rail, relatively unknown until September, successfully tender for the provision of traction for the operation of Railhead Treatment Trains (RHTT) in the West Country, using two refurbished Class 47/7s bought from EWS, Nos:

47727 'Rebecca'   47749 ' Demelza'

Colas, the French infrastructure company part of Amey Seco, will run RHTTs along with DRS, EWS and Jarvis (MPV only) and have two initial diagrams:

3S11, Par - Par via Plymouth and Hackney Yard   (Mon. to Fri. + Sun)

3S12, Par - Par via Penzance   (Sun. to Fri.)

(Previous Page) : On Thursday, 27th September, the two Colas Rail 47s top 'n' tail a special 6Z47, 13:56 Exeter Depot - Penzance RHTT past Aller Junction, Newton Abbott, with No 47727 'Rebecca' leading, resplendent in Colas yellow, orange and black livery.   (Robert Sherwood)

ENTERPRISE

Stanton Grove Newsprint

Late in 2006, but too late to report in the previous edition, Knowsley rail terminal (located on the Kirkby - Wigan Wallgate line) ceased receiving goods by rail; one notable casualty being the daily newsprint service from Immingham. However, the newsprint flow switches to a new terminal in Liverpool Docks, Stanton Grove, by way of a new 'trip' working from Arpley Yard, Warrington; the full diagram is:

6M30, 20:35 Immingham - Arpley

6F13, 04:36 Arpley - Stanton Grove

6F14, 09:30 Stanton Grove - Arpley

6E33, 13:51 Arpley - Immingham

(Above) : Class 67 No 67006 'Special Messenger' rounds Winwick curve en route to Warrington on 23rd March and upon arrival the Cargowaggons will go forward on 6E33, Arpley - Immingham, while the locomotive will work 6F10, Arpley - Liverpool Gladstone Dock loaded steel.   (Fred Kerr)

AUTOMOTIVE

New 'IPAs'

(Below) : This is a fairly new addition to the freight working timetable; 6Z46, the 10:52 (SO) Halewood - Southampton Eastern Docks loaded car train. However, it is the train itself, with 2 new STVA IPA wagons (design code IPE919, Pool 0324) which is of interest, rather than the motive power. No 66225 is in charge on Saturday, 21st April, passing Berkswell en-route to Southampton via Coventry, Leamington Spa, Oxford and, after Didcot, via Chippenham due to engineering work on the normal route via Reading and Basingstoke.   (Peter Tandy)

INTERMODAL

Victa Westlink Rail

Victa Westlink Rail launch a new Anglo-Scottish intermodal service using the safety case it inherited from FM Rail and hire in two DRS Class 66/4s for the operation. The train initially uses Mega 3 'Pocket' wagons (coded KAA), originally purchased for Blue Circle 'Piggyback' trains in 2003 (See *Freightmaster Review*, page 127 for details), but later use IKA 'Megafret' wagons to enable a wider range of containers to be conveyed. After initial trials, the service becomes:

4L94, 09:05 Ditton - Purfleet	MWFO
4M89, 18:10 Purfleet - Ditton	MWFO
4S03, 00:10 Ditton - Grangemouth	TThO
4M94, 21:45 Grangemouth - Ditton	TThO

Unfortunately, this service is axed in October due to poor loadings but, during its working life, proves to be a magnet for railway photographers and a selection of four contrasting images can be seen overleaf.

(Above) : The next four images depict the Victa Westlink intermodal services at various stages of their respective southbound journey on the WCML. To begin, No 66414 heads a well loaded 4M94, 12:35 Grangemouth - Crewe on 1st October in the Upper Clyde Valley at Crawford, six miles north of Beattock Summit. Note the well known landmark of the 'T' shape conifer plantation on the hillside. (Donald Cameron)

(Below) : Prior to being retimed to leave Grangemouth nine hours earlier and a change of destination, No 66418 stands at Preston in the early morning hours of 7th July (03:45 to be precise!) with 4M94, the 21:45 Grangemouth - Ditton intermodal. (Martin Harkness)

(Above) : On 3rd May, a pair of DRS Class 66/4 locomotives head along the 'Up' fast line on the WCML at Cow Roast, Tring, with a Victa Railfreight service, running on this occasion as 4L94, Grangemouth - Purfleet. The KAA 'Pocket' wagons can clearly be seen behind Nos 66417 + 66419. It was to be hoped that healthier payloads would follow, but alas not and the service is axed five months later. (David Stracey)

(Below) : An interesting and colourful pairing materialises on 3rd August when the two hire locomotives are from separate operators. GBRf No 66710 and DRS No 66418 head 4L94, Ditton - Purfleet on 3rd August through Harrow & Wealdstone station on the 'Up' slow line. (Justin Buckley)

'PLASTERBOARD EXPRESS'

Perhaps, not quite as headline-grabbing as the Tesco Express, but another, jus as innovative service is launched by DRS in July, conveying plasterboard from the British Gypsum works at Kirkby Thore (Newbiggin) on the Settle and Carlisle line, to Elderslie near Paisley. Both trains run via Motherwell and Beattock:

4S39, 00:34 Newbiggin - Elderslie

4M78, 14:02 Elderslie   - Newbiggin

(Opposite) : On 1st October, No 66419 passes Wandel Mill, three miles north of Abington, with 4M78, Elderslie - Newbiggin plasterboard empties. The train is made up of 'Megafrets' on which 'Curtainsiders' (swapbodies) are mounted, many wearing British Gypsum logo and corporate colours. (Donald Cameron)

METALS

Swindon Steel

Yes, that's right, steel at Swindon! After months of taking in steel by road and a couple of trial workings the new steel terminal at Swindon finally starts receiving regular rail-bourne shipments, the first timetabled service runs on Tuesday, 4th September.

The steel is for Mini car panel production at the BMW plant in Swindon. The traffic originates from Goole and is forwarded by existing services to Newport Alexandra Dock Junction (6V19, Doncaster - Margam) from where it reaches Swindon on a new trip working:

6C01, 08:26 Newport ADJ - Swindon   TFO   Q

6C02, 17:06 Swindon - Newport ADJ   TFO   Q

The loaded train propels into the terminal and the empties run round in Cocklebury yard, but the finished panels are regrettably moved to BMW Cowley, Oxford, by road!

(Above) : On the first day, No 66220 propels 6C01, Newport ADJ - Swindon and its train of loaded steel into the single road terminal consisting of BIA, BXA and BYA steel carrying wagons. It may well be a first for BIA and BXA wagons at Swindon, these mainly work steel flows between Wolverhampton / Doncaster and Goole / Immingham. It is also interesting to ponder how planning permission could be granted for such an ugly looking building in close proximity to the former 'listed' buildings of the former GWR railway works and why isn't the steel being brought directly into the BMW plant via Highworth Junction? (Martin Buck)

DIVERSIONS

GRAYRIGG DERAILMENT

On 3 February, Pendolino set No 390033 'City of Glasgow' derails near Grayrigg, between Oxenholme and Tebay, at some 95mph, while working the 17:15 London Euston - Glasgow Central, after passing over a crossover at Lambrigg.

The leading unit turns through 180 degrees, the second lying on the embankment and the remaining vehicles straddling the embankment. Miraculously, the death toll amounted to only one.

As a result of this incident, Anglo-Scottish freight services are diverted via the Cumbrian Coast, Settle & Carlisle and ECML.

(Above) : There is no 'booked' freight over the Hellifield - Blackburn route, save when diversions off the WCML are in force, like Grayrigg derailment, for example. On 8th March, No 66530 heads 6M11 through Clitheroe, the diverted 06:06 Hunterston - Fiddlers Ferry power station loaded HHAs. (Fred Kerr)

(Below) A pair of Class 86/6 locomotives No 86637 + No 86614, both sporting the old Freightliner grey livery, enter Newcastle Central station on 8th March with the diverted 4L89, Coatbridge - Felixstowe 'liner. (Carl Gorse)

(Above) : On a very wet and gloomy day on the Settle & Carlisle, 'Eddie The Engine' (No 66411) approaches Kirkby Stephen station on 28th February with the diverted 4S43, 'Tesco Express'.

(Below) : A plume of exhaust trails from Class 37/4 No 37406 'The Saltire Society' and onto Ribblehead viaduct as the 37 proceeds at a leisurely pace south with the diverted 6K05, Carlisle Yard - Crewe 'Virtual Quarry' departmental on St. David's Day, 1st March. (Both Andrew Naylor)

(Above) : The 'Malcolm' train (4M30, Grangemouth - Daventry) is seen heading south through Derby on 6 March on No 66407 + No 66402 (dit) in charge, running around 5 hours late on this particular occasion.
(Ralf Edge)

(Below) : No 66425 heads 4S43, Daventry - Grangemouth' Tesco Express' away from Healey Mills on 26th February, shortly before Tesco decide the additional journey time running via Diggle and the ECML is unacceptable.
(Ian Ball)

EAST COAST DIVERSIONS

(Above) : 'Grayrigg' necessitates Anglo-Scottish sleepers to be diverted via the ECML. On 9th April, Nos 67005 'Queen's Messenger' + 67006 'Royal Sovereign' assist No 90034 on 1M16, the diverted 20:40 Inverness - Euston sleeper, seen crossing the River Nene at Peterborough. The 67s have been added at Peterborough for the journey over the non-electrified Tottenham & Hampstead Joint Line.

(Top Left) : Engineering work on the ECML south of Doncaster results in services being diverted via Lincoln to Newark and even Spalding. On 20th January, 4L85 Leeds - Ipswich Yard freightliner is routed via Spalding, where it is seen headed by Nos 66714 + 66721 + 66718 and the failed train engine No 66537.

(Bottom) Left) : On 7th February, No 66724 passes Swinderby (between Lincoln and Newark) with the diverted 4L78, Selby - Felixstowe intermodal. Note, the local mileposts denoting 25 miles from Nottingham.

(Below) : The awful flooding experienced in Yorkshire this summer causes major disruption to rail services and on 2nd July, 4O90 Doncaster - Thamesport intermodal is routed away from its normal route of Tamwoth - Bescot - Rugby and onto the ECML. No. 56303 passes Holme, near Peterborough. (All John Rudd)

DIVERSIONS

ELY DERAILMENT

On 22nd June, 6L58, Mountsorrel - Chelmsford self-discharge train hauled by No 60068 derails near Soham, blocking the line between Ely Dock Junction and Chippenham Junction. With 11 wagons derailed on the single line bridge over the River Ouse, the bridge will have to be replaced, resulting in trains to/from Stowmarket being diverted; most Freightliners running via the ECML and North London, other services via Cambridge.

(Above) : On Saturday, 20th October, No 66539 heads the diverted 4E49, Felixstowe - York Holgate freightliner past Devil's Dyke, between Newmarket and Dullingham, on the single line linking Newmarket and Cambridge. Upon reaching Cambridge, the train will reverse and proceed to Ely in order to regain the booked route.

(Below) : No 66541 and a fully laden 4L85 pass under Ferme Park Flyover on the 'Up' goods line at Harringay on 18th July. The train is heading for Finsbury Park, where it will leave the ECML and proceed onto the North London Line, thence to Stratford and on into East Anglia. (Both Nick Slocombe)

BASINGSTOKE BLOCKADE

Network Rail prepare for a 10-day closure of all lines through Basingstoke starting on Good Friday (6 April). It is the key element of a £130m resignalling project to replace equipment fitted in the 1960s. There are a total of 270 new signals, 100km of new track and 81 sets of points, not too mention a new signalling centre at Basingstoke. The closure affects all services on the routes from London to Salisbury & Exeter and from London to Southampton, plus the busy link between Basingstoke and Reading. Consequently, freight services to/from Southampton are being diverted via the Wyle Valley.

(Above) : On Thursday, 12th April a Class 67 makes a rare appearance on an EWS Intermodal working when No 67003 is allocated to work 4O36, Hams Hall - Southampton. The late running service is seen on the Westbury - Salisbury main line passing Upton Scudamore. (Don Gatehouse)

(Top) : An interesting combination .... No 66226 + No 60060 'James Watt' head a very late running and lightweight 6O12, Carlisle Yard - Eastleigh 'Enterprise' on Friday, 13th April, at Little Langford. (Martin Blois)

'Murco' Divert

(Top Left) : On 5th April, 6E55, Theale - Lindsey tanks run with No 60068 'Charles Darwin' in charge and a rake of red MURCO tanks from 6A11, Robeston - Theale. This working is a result of a forthcoming blockade on the South Wales main line, whereby Robeston refinery would not be accessible by 6B33. The tanks are sent to Lindsey for reloading to avoid a shortage of fuel at Theale. The very unusual consist for the area is seen climbing Hatton Bank. (Peter Tandy)

(Bottom Left) : Due to engineering work between Cam and Stonehouse over the May Day Bank Holiday, 6B13, Robeston - Westerleigh loaded petroleum tanks is diverted via Severn Tunnel and Bristol Parkway. The train works in top 'n' tail formation involving No 60025 'Caledonian Paper' and No 60092 'Reginald Munns', necessitating a reverse at Yate onto the oil terminal branch line. The ensemble is seen at Westerleigh Junction. (Richard Giles)

Erewash Blockade

(Right) : Major resignalling work in the Erewash Valley sees freight services diverted via Derby and Freightliner's No 57002 'Freightliner Phoenix' acts as 'Thunderbird' on 8th July, stabled at Derby. (Ralf Edge)

(Below) : No 60500 'Rail Magazine' sweeps round the curve at Pride Park, Derby, on 13th June with the diverted 6M87, Ely - Peak Forest empty HOA hoppers. (Paul Biggs)

DIVERSIONS

THAMES VALLEY FLOODING

(Above) : It first starts in Yorkshire with heavy rain, 'Monsoon' like, causing major disruptions to ECML train services followed in late July/early August when yet more heavy rain causes flooding in Gloucestershire and Warwickshire, the Thames Valley, and with it more rail chaos. Two Thames Valley diversions are depicted here starting with No 57006 'Freightliner Reliance' heading east along the Great Western Mainline at Taplow on 23rd July in charge of the diverted 4S59, Southampton - Coatbridge freightliner.   (Martin Blois)

(Below) : Meanwhile, a contrast of old and new rolling stock greets the cameraman awaiting the arrival of the Avon 'Binliner' at Aylesbury on Friday, 27th July. Having departed from Calvert somewhat earlier than previous days, No 66609 is held north of Aylesbury until a path becomes available for the diverted 4V60, Calvert - Bath/Bristol. It is now passing the Chiltern Railways depot at Aylesbury, where DMU No 168 109 is waiting to proceed into the station and "Bubble Car" No 121 020 is stabled.   (Geoff Plumb)

PEGGED OUT!

This section takes a look at infrastucture and a selection of photographs featuring some interesting departmental 'trips' and, to begin, a brief glimpse of locations which are photogenic from a 'semaphorial' perspective!

Helsby

(Above) : On the last day of July, No 57303 'Alan Tracy' approaches Helsby with 6J37, Carlisle Yard - Chirk loaded logs, conveyed in both converted IGA and KFA wagons. The two signals on the left are relatively new, replacing the previous ones on the site, as illustrated on Page 40 of 'Railfreight Yearbook - 2005'.   (Martin Buck)

Gilberdyke

(Above) : Gilberdyke is where the line from Doncaster joins the main line from Hull to Selby and Leeds. On 26th April, 'Shed' No 66124 approaches Gilberdyke from the east on 26th April with 6D72, Hull Dairycoates - Rylstone empty 'Tilcon' hoppers.

(Below) : On the same date, No 66563 passes Gilberdyke Junction on the approach to the station with 4H31, the 09:45 Sudforth Lane Sidings - Hull Docks empty coal hoppers. (Both Geoff Plumb)

Pinxton

(Below) : A fine composition - semaphores and signalbox. At a bitterly cold Pinxton on 6th February, No 47828 'Joe Strummer' passes light engine, running as 0Z37, Derby RTC - Thoresby Junction Serco train.　　(Mick Tindall)

Wymondham

(Above) : On 21st April, Class 57/6 No 57601 leads the Green Express 'Fenlands Cathedral & Sunrise Coast Explorer' past Wymondham South Junction on the approach to the scheduled stop at Wymondham, running as 1Z22, Ely - Great Yarmouth. The train originates from Mills Hill.　　(James Welham)

DEPARTMENTAL TURNS

EWS

Aller Divergence

(Left) : On Wednesday, 11th April, Class 60s No 60019 + No 60060 'James Watt' (nearest the camera) top 'n' tail 6W73, the 16:46 Westbury – St Blazey spoil train past Aller Junction.

The train is on the main line to Plymouth and the other two lines on the left 'diverge' to Torquay and Paignton.   (Robert Sherwood)

Cambrian 'Trips'

(Top Right) : A splendid contrast of colour shows off this image of No 37406 'The Saltire Society' on 29th April passing Upton hauling Network Rail and Railtrack-branded auto-ballasters, which form 6W66, the 17:14 Bescot - Bescot via Pwllheli. This was during a spell when 37s regularly turn out on Cambrian ballast trains.   (Ralf Edge)

(Bottom Right) : During February, several continuous welded rail and ballast trains visit the Cambrian Line, as evident in this panoramic view of No 66107 inching across the newly-laid track at Aberdovey, while returning to Machynlleth, having finished dropping the track panels and then running round at Tywyn.   (Richard Jones)

Robin Hood Line

(Below) : The Robin Hood Line seldom receives photographic consideration, probably due in some small part in there being little or no 'non-shed' loco-hauled activity over the line. On 24th June, No 66189 departs from Kirkby In Ashfield station with 6B15, Kirkby Lane End - Toton Engineers train as part of the areas resignalling & track improvment scheme.   (Mick Tindall)

Dunston Tractors (*Above*) : Nos 37422 'Cardiff Canton' + 37406 'The Saltire Society' are seen working 6W28, the 23:30 Bescot - Bescot via Shrewsbury, and Crewe travelling south through Swan Lane, Dunston, on 29th April. (Ralf Edge)

Spoil Sport! (*Below*) : A superb view of Leeds Midland Road on 15th April and a depot crammed with FHH Class 66 locomotives and HHA wagons. No 37405 pases on 15th April with 6T79, Whitehall Junction - Healey Mills loaded spoil train. (Ian Ball)

GBRf

Capital Locations

(Above) : On 17th April, the colourful combination of 'Metronet' No 66722 ' Sir Edward Watkin' + 'Medite' No 66709 'Joseph Arnold Davies' head 6O61, Ferme Park - Grain through Kensington Olympia station, consisting of 10 Metronet Autoballasters. (James Welham)

(Below) : Meanwhile, we venture north to Junction Road Junction, which is located between Harringay and Gospel Oak, to view No 66719 'Metro-Land' passing on 16th April with 6M66, the 11:17 Ferme Park - Wellingboro formed of empty Metronet MLA bogie wagons. (Nigel Gibbs)

Off The Beaten Track ....

(Above) : On a damp and gloomy 24th February, No 66708 'Joseph Arnold Davies' heads along the Chiltern Line at Wendover, alongside the A413 road, with 6M65, Ferme Park - Mantles Wood ballast. (Martin Blois)

(Below) : During the weekend of 5th/6th May there is a blockade of the Braintree branch with several departmental trains visiting the six-mile long branch line; No 66705 'Golden Jubilee' stands on the approach to Cressing station with a train of FEA flat wagons waiting to take away the removed track panels. (James Welham)

FHH

Drain Train

(Above) : Drainage is a key element of track maintenance, but can be a difficult issue to tackle, so the 'Drain Train' offers a practical and effective solution to trackside drain maintenance on the rail network. No 66605 passes through Rugby on 25th March with 6Y70, the 09:35 Weedon - Nuneaton - Bletchley 'Drain Train'.   (Andy Small)

Mix 'n' Match

(Below) : An odd combination ..... Freightliner's No 66583 passes Abington loops on the WCML at 08:42hrs on the morning of 24th July with 6P29, Carlisle - Millerhill departmental, formed of a rake of EWS low sided bogie box wagons ('Carkind' codes MCA / MDA and MOA).   (Keith McGovern)

NETWORK RAIL

(Above) : This is one of the rarest of loco-hauled workings photographed during daylight hours as, other than nocturnal winter de-icing duties, the Network Rail Class 73s spend the rest of the year dormant in Tonbridge West Yard (or running light engine to St Leonards for refuelling). The NR-owned EDs No 73212 + No 73213 approach Sevenoaks on 22nd September hauling thirteen loaded Falcons, forming 6G14, the 14:00 Staines - Tonbridge West Yard, this being only the second freight working in 2007 for the yellow EDs! (Marc Ely)

(Below) : Meanwhile, on 30th August, the duo are seen again, but this time at Derby, running as 5Z73, the 17:00 Grove Park - Barrow Hill, transferring two GLVs to Barrow Hill for 'work' to be undertaken. These GLVs are used as de-icing vehicles on the former Southern Region. (Ralf Edge)

S. & C. BLOCKADE

(Above) : For a fortnight in July, the Settle & Carlisle line shuts to allow track renewals to take place in the Crosby Garrett and Ribblehead areas, during which a total of seven Class 60s will be be deployed on engineers trains. No 60029 'Clitheroe Castle' waits at Waitby on 9th July with 6L11, Appleby - Carlisle loaded ballast, prior to entering the engineering possession.

(Below) : On the same day, one of Freightliner's fleet of Class 66/6s, No 66618, crosses Arten Gill viaduct after leaving an engineers possession with 6Y06, Blea Moor - Crewe Basford Hall, formed of MRA bogie side tipping ballast wagons.   (Both Ian Ball)

Class 31

(Above) : The venerable Class 31 locomotives, whilst having no mandated freight duties, are still to be found around the network on test trains, such as we see here at Melton Mowbray. The distinctive network Rail yellow liveried pairing of No 31105 + No 31602 top 'n' tail 4Q07, the 08:56 Derby RTC - Old Dalby test train on 1st May; these trains being allocated a 'Q' headcode when required to stay on booked route / line. (Nigel Gibbs)

(Below) : Meanwhile, on 30th August, No 31459 'Cerebus' is a most unusual choice of motive power for the Birkenhead North - Crewe Merseyrail unit transfer - the Class 507/508 EMUs are experiencing excessive wear, necessitating wheel re-profiling at Crewe. The ensemble, inclusive of EMU Nos 507.013 + 507.015 is seen in the suburbs of Birkenhead at Upton and the M55 motorway is partially visible in the background. (Fred Kerr)

6M33

(Above) : This could qualify for the 37's ' Working of the Year' when, after arriving in South Wales on a railtour, Nos 37406 'The Saltire Society' + 37422 'Cardiff Canton' are unusually allocated to work 6M33, Avonmouth - Wembley 'Enterprise' on 14th May in place of the normal Class 67. In fading light, the pair are seen storming past Highworth Junction, Swindon, 50 minutes early. In fact, this is believed to be only the second time 6M33 has been worked by a 37 since the working started in September 2002; the other occasion being on 14th April 2003 when No 37670 'St. Blazey TR&S Depot worked the train.   (Martin Buck)

6M05 - To The Rescue!

(Below) : Due to no crew being available at Scunthorpe for No 60082 'Mam Tor' on 6M05, Roxby - Northenden GMRC empty 'Binliner' on 11th July, two 37s No 37410 'Aluminium 100' + No 37422 'Cardiff Canton' are summoned to work the train forward, Class 60 and all. The pair having been originally booked to run light engine to Healey Mills. The train is seen approaching Hatfield & Stainforth station.   (Rob Terrace)

37087

(Above) : This locomotive is the last 'split box' 37 on the network and is a popular target for rail photographers and on 12th March, the DRS machine is an unusual choice of motive power for 6Z37, the 13:30 Doncaster Decoy - Bescot departmental, seen approaching Burton-on-Trent.   (Ralf Edge)

(Below) : On 6th January, No 37087 it is seen stabled overnight at York with the Norwich Union Wheel providing a spectacular illumination in the background.   (Carl Gorse)

Overleaf :

CLASS 57 TWILIGHT

As a result of a new batch of Class 66/5 locomotives arriving in April, Freightliner start taking some Class 57s out of traffic and return them to Portebrook, although some re-appear later working for DRS on RHTTs! On 1st May, Nos 57007 - 57010 and No 57012 are placed in store and a tribute to this Class is made with two superb night-time images taken at Southampton Maritime Freightliner Terminal on 16th May by Carl Gorse.

(Page 60) : 57002 'Freightliner Phoenix'   *(Page 61)* : 57004 'Freightliner Quality'

LOCOMOTIVES

TORNESS FLASKS

(Above) : Moving north of the border into Scotland, the spotlight falls on the flow of nuclear flasks between Carlisle and Torness nuclear power station and the interesting use of motive power and running practice. On 4th October, two immaculate DRS Class 47 locomotives No 47802 + No 47501 approach Prestonpans with 6S43, Carlisle Kingmoor - Torness, and will run to Grantshouse in order to gain access to the power station.

(Below) : However, in order to eliminate a run-round manouevre at Grantshouse, the return working operates in top 'n' tail formation as we see in this view of No 37515 + 4 FNA wagons + No 37194 (rear) working 6M50, Torness - Carlisle on 21st August passing Wester Hailes, on the Edinburgh - Carstairs main line, shortly after top 'n' tail running commences. (Both Keith McGovern)

HAPPY BIRTHDAY FASTLINE

One year on and still going strong.... *Fastline* - a subsidiary of Jarvis - entered the railfreight market on 8th May 2006, running an out & back intermodal service from Thamesport to Doncaster, closely followed by a second service to Birch Coppice. Three ex-EWS Class 56 locomotives were overhauled and repainted in Fastline colours (Nos. 56301 / 302 / 303) to provide the traction, although No 56303 did not see as much service as the other two 'Grids.

(Top) : On 18th April, No 56303 passes Cheddington with 4O90, Doncaster - Thamesport. (Anthony Kay)

(Above) : Meanwhile, a rare working for a Fastline 'Grid' is recorded on 13th February, when No 56303 is seen again, but at Whittlesea in charge of a return departmental working from Whitemoor to Doncaster. (John Rudd)

47811

(Above) : On 11th July, No 47811 has the distinction of becoming the first Class 47 locomotive to work 6M80, Dagenham - Calvert loaded 'Binliner' in 2007, seen at Princes Risborough on the Chiltern Line. (David Stracey)

47832

(Opposite) : No 47832 is the first locomotive to display Victa Westlink Rail livery after being outshopped from Barrow Hill and is seen at Derby the following day, 14th June. The loco then moves south to the West Somerset Railway where it will be on display for two weeks. (Paul Biggs)

47501

(Below) : With 3,580hp at their disposal DRS Class 47/4 No 47501 and Class 20/3 No 20302 make an interesting combination as they power an additional 6L74, 09:18 Willesden - Sizewell nuclear flasks service through Colchester on 26th March. (John Binch)

OUT & ABOUT .... with W.C.R.C

(Above) : The heavily delayed 5Z47, 13:24 Stewarts Lane - Tyseley stock move conveying inoperational No 37248 and a set of coaching stock going to Tyseley for tyre turning passes Hatton North Junction on 24th August with No 47245 hauling the ensemble. Both locos are resplendent in matching West Coast Railway Company maroon livery. The rear coach had severe flats and was making quite a noise as it passed at 19:22hrs. 5Z47 left Stewarts Lane in excess of 2 hours late, and that lateness grew almost exponentially; any later the shadows visible in the foreground would encroach on the track and spoil the shot.

(Below) : On 18th July, the inspection saloon named 'Amanda' runs from Derby to Stratford-upon-Avon and then on to Shrewsbury and Birkenhead. The outward run (2Z01) to Stratford is via the North Warwickshire Line and the saloon, headed by WCRC's No 47854, is seen entering Henley-in-Arden and even though the light is on the "wrong" side, the infrastructure at the station makes up for the less than ideal lighting.   (Both Peter Tandy)

SIXTY 60s

In previous years, the start of a new fiscal period heralds a period of storage for a number of Class 60s as a result of reduced demand during the summer months.

However, 2007 proves to be an exception, due entirely to the ever increasing number of Class 66/0s being used in France, so fewer 'Tugs' are stored.

By the end of May, the situation is healthier with a total of 60 Class 60s in active service.

(Above) : Nowadays, Selby is somewhat off the main freight trunk routes, but was once a busy bottleneck on the ECML prior to the building of the 'Selby Diversion.' Loadhaul-liveried No 60059 'Swinden Dalesman' passes through the station on 6th March with 6D72, Hull Dairycoates - Rylstone limestone empties. (Ian Ball)

(Above) : This train is 6V17, the 16:32 Bescot - Portbury which earlier forms a service from Fidlers Ferry Power Station. Its booked traction is an EWS Class 66 but, on 2nd August, a 60 is in charge, giving the rare chance to photograph one on HTA hoppers. No 60056 'William Beveridge' is seen where the main line comes out of the wood at Croome Perry, fortunately just as the sun decides to break through the clouds. (Peter Tandy)

Overleaf :

(Page 68 - Top Left) : The Theale to Lindsey tanks (6E55) with No 60500 'Rail Magazine' at the front is seen on 6th April a few yards to the north of Warwick Parkway station, on the climb of Hatton Bank, with a dead hen pheasant on the buffer beam. Prominent in the background are the Round Tower of Warwick Castle and the tall tower of St. Mary's Church. The architectural slendour of Warwick contrasts nicely with the abandoned shopping trolley in the bottom right-hand corner. (Peter Tandy)

(Bottom Left) : In glorious morning sunshine on 10th March, No 60063 'James Murray' is seen again heading 6B42, Toton - Forders departmental service at Frisby; note the newly fitted mirrors. (Mick Tindall)

(Page 69) : On 5th June, No 60063 'James Murray' proceeds along the 'Up' Hope Valley Line at New Mills South Junction working 6H01, Oakleigh - Tunstead BLI limestone empties; the train proceeds to Chinley North Junction, thence the 'freight only' line via Dove Holes Tunnel and Peak Forest to Tunstead. (Fred Kerr)

LOCOMOTIVES

MORE IMPORTS ....

During the first six months of the year, Freightliner add to their ever-growing fleet of locomotives by taking delivery of 16 new locomotives in three batches, thus:

      66623 - 66625   66582 - 66586   66587 - 66594

DRS and First GBRf will also take delivery of new Class 66s during the year.

(Above) : On 23rd March, No 66625 heads south at Wellingborough with a rake of new HIA bogie aggregate hoppers, running as 6M17, Croft - Neasden.   (Martin Buck)

Blue is the Colour ....

(Above) : No 66623 is repainted in Bardon blue and is the first Class 66 to be completely customer branded. The locomotive carrries Bardon mid blue with Freightliner green roof and is in celebration of the rail operator's gain from EWS of the Bardon aggregate traffic in April 2006. On 14th March, No 66623 passes through Leicester heading 6C70, Mountsorrel - Luton loaded stone, formed of MJA bogie wagons, many of which have been attacked by the so called grafitti artists!

(Below) : Further south, the locomotive is seen passing Kilby Bridge Junction with empty JGA hoppers on 6th April, running as 6M54, Thorney Mil - Bardon Hill.   (Both Andy Small)

FIRST GB RAILFREIGHT - TAKE 5

66723 - 66727

On 8th January, First Group's freight business, GB Railfreight, show off their new batch of Class 66/7 locomotives outside Wembley Heavy Repair Shop, resplendent in a new corporate livery. At the presentation at Wembley depot, GBRf Managing Director, John Smith, reviews a successful 2006 for the Company, as a result of winning new traffic, especially the Metronet track renewal programme. Two of the locomotives are to be dedicated to the new Tyne Dock - Drax coal flow; the remainder being available for new coal flows, hire and stock movements. In fact, the first working for a member of the new additions takes place on 13th January when No. 66727 works 5Z82, Derby Litchurch Lane - Laira stock move of refurbished Mk. 3 vehicles.

(Above) : At the presentation, Nos. 66727 to 66723 line up for the official photographs with a splendid backdrop, the new Wembley Stadium.   (Brian Morrison)

LOCOMOTIVES

66723

(Above) : The first of four images to illustrate the diversity of GBRf's traffic and No 66723 easing past St Vigeans (Near Arbroath) on 15th May with 6S60, Harwich - Aberdeen Guild Street 'Mud oil' tanks; the first visit of a 'Barbie' to Aberdeen.   (Jim Ramsay)

66725

(Previous Page) : In the early days following their introduction, No 66725 is a well-photographed machine, judging by the number of images submitted for this publication. A notable submission being this one of No 66725 approaching Hemel Hempstead on 16th March, dragging a failed Freightliner Class 57 No 57002 'Freightliner Phoenix' on 4L41, Daventry - Felixstowe freightliner; a truly impressive close-up view!   (Nigel Gibbs)

66724

(Below) : A rarely photographed location, the freight-only Grain branch, which gives access from Hoo Junction to Grain and Thamesport. No 66724 prepares to leave Grain with 6M71, the 22.00 Grain - Wellingborough ballast, scheduled to leave the previous day but delayed until 16:00hrs on 13th March due to derailed wagons.   (Jonathan Makepeace)

66726

(Above) : No 66726 powers 6E96, Bury St. Edmunds - Peterborough empty stone train at Ely Dock Junction on 14th March, a duty normally worked by an EWS Class 66/0 locomotive. (Anthony Kay)

66727

(Below) : The new locos see regular work on stock transfers between Derby and Plymouth, such as on 8th August when No 66727 hauls a rake of HST vehicles to be refurbished, running as 5Z90, the 07:53 Laira - Derby Litchurch Lane. The train is unusually routed via the 'Berks & Hants' and is seen above the Kennet & Avon Canal passing Crofton pumping station. (Martin Buck)

LOCOMOTIVES

Class 67s - Finding Work!

(Above) : Apart from charter train work, it is pleasing to see the under-utilised Class 67 fleet finding more work on freight flows around the country, mostly on short distance 'trips.' On 15th March, No. 67007 approaches Purfleet with 6L35, Wembley - Purfleet intermodal, running alongside the new CTRL. *(Anthony Kay)*

(Below) : Peak Forest aggregate flows operated by EWS are the preserve of the Class 60, save for the odd 66, so you can imagine the surprise when a Class 67 turns up! On Saturday, 28th July, No 67003 unexpectedly works 6M87, Ely - Peak Forest empty stone hoppers and is pictured passing Ollerbrook, just east of Edale, in the heart of the Derbyshire Dales. *(Justin Buckley)*

LOCOMOTIVE PROFILE

Class 90

The Class 90 locomotives were the last to be ordered before sectorisation of British Rail in the 1980s; built for both passenger and freight services at Crewe Works between 1987 and 1990.

For such a small fleet, they carry an assortment of liveries, as illustrated here.

RfD Two Tone Grey

(Top Left) : On 23rd October, No 90036 complete with EWS 'Beasties' sticker waits to depart Ipswich with the 13:00 Norwich - Liverpool Street. (Martin Buck)

EWS Maroon & Gold

(Centre) : No 90020 sits atop DVT No 82128 at Manchester Piccadilly prior to departing with the 15:24hrs service to Birmingham New Street on 10th January. (Carl Gorse)

Freightliner Green

(Previous Page) : On 16th March, No 90041 leads 4M87, Felixstowe - Trafford Park past Rivenhall foot crossing. (James Welham)

Freightliner Grey

(Below) : No 90048 sporting Freightliner two-tone grey with black cab doors & window surrounds, plus red triangle logo, eases 4M87 out of Ipswich Yard and into the station on 23rd October. (Martin Buck)

'One'

(Above) : The Anglia 'One' colour scheme is carried by Class 90 locomotives working passenger expresses between London Liverpool Street and Norwich. The main colour is slate-blue, with the locomotive ends featuring bold 'rainbow stripes' of magenta, yellow, slate-blue, turquoise and pale-blue. No 90004, complete with matching Mark 3 coaches, arrives at Ipswich station on 23rd October with the 12:00 Norwich - Liverpool Street. (Martin Buck)

First 'Scotrail' Blue

(Below) : On 2nd March, while on his way to work, the photographer captures No 90024 passing Harringay with 1M16, the diverted 20:40 Inverness - London Euston Scotrail sleeper.   (Nick Slocombe)

'FAREWELL TO THY GREATNESS'   *January 1982*

A quarter of a century ago, 2nd January 1982, the end befell one of the most iconic classes of diesel locomotives to ever grace Britain's railways, when British Rail switched off its last Class 55 'Deltic'. Who could ever forget the scene on that memorable day with thousands of enthusiasts, and ITN news crew, at King's Cross station to commemorate the end, as No. 55022 'Royal Scots Grey' (quite fitting 'Royal Scots Grey' being the longest serving member of the class) came to rest on the blocks with the 'Deltic Scotsman Farewell' charter.

A total of 22 Deltics were built between 1961-1962 and were named after famous regiments or racehorses and during their working life were allocated to Finsbury Park, Gateshead, Haymarket and York depots. Fortunately, seven members of the class have found a second lease of life in preservation. So, four images to enjoy as a tribute.

(Above) : One of the most picturesque settings on the ECML runs for about eight miles north out of Berwick-upon-Tweed where the main line skirts the North Sea. On 3rd June 1978, high above the cliffs, No 55019 'Royal Highland Fusilier' passes Lamberton with the 10:53 London King's Cross - Edinburgh.

(Top Left) : On 26th May, No 55012 'Crepello' passes High Dyke, near Grantham, with the 15:25 Leeds - King's Cross - how different the ECML looks today with all the paraphernalia of electrification!

(Bottom Left) : Here, a classic view looking down on Newcastle Central station from the Castle Keep and No 55007 'Pinza' departing past the famous diamond crossover with the 10:00 London King's Cross - Edinburgh; the 'Flying Scotsman' - probably the most famous named train in the world!

(Below) : On 23rd August 1978, No 55017 ' The Durham Light Infantry' approaches 'London 350 miles' signpost at Grantshouse while in charge of the 09:00 Aberdeen - King's Cross.   (All Hugh Ballantyne)

'WESTERN TRIBUTE'

February 1977

Thirty years ago on 26th February 1977, the final British Rail-organised trip with Class 52 traction ran from London Paddington to Swansea and Plymouth & back, featuring Nos D1013 'Western Ranger' + D1023 'Western Fusilier', all for a modest ticket price of £15 first class or £10 second class!

The 'Westerns' were the last class of Western Region hydraulic locomotives to be built. The first locomotive of the type D1000 'Western Enterprise' arrived in November 1961 in a stunning livery of 'Desert Sand' with two bogies, each with three axles, all of which were driven. The unique design of the 'Westerns' oozed elegance, gaining immediate affection among enthusiasts and argueably became the best looking locomotive to ever run on BR.

A total of 74 'Westerns' were built between 1961 - 1964 at either Swindon or Crewe, thus:

D1000 - D1029 Swindon   D1030 - D1073   Crewe

Within the class, there have been five different liveries (Blue, Desert Sand, Golden Ochre, Green, Maroon) and an individuality by virtue of the fact that each had its own name prefixed by the word 'Western', by which the class has been referred to by enthusiasts ever since. They were the principle passenger express locomotive on the Western Region until the mid 1970s, when displaced by Class 50s from the London Midland Region, and relegated to secondary passenger services and freight turns. The final four members of the class were 'switched off' on 28th February 1977 but, pleasingly, seven survive into preservation:

D1010 Western Campaigner   D1013 Western Ranger   D1015 Western Champion

D1023 Western Fusilier   D1041 Western Prince   D1048 Western Lady

D1062 Western Courier

(Above) : On her old stomping ground, No D1024 'Western Huntsman' speeds through Oldfield Park, Bath, on 5th September 1970 hauling the 12:45 Paddington - Weston Super Mare.

(Top Right) : A contrast of liveries and a close up view of a 'Western' on shed. On 1st November 1969, BR-Blue liveried No D1014 'Western Leviathan' idles away the time at Bristol Bath Road TMD along with maroon No D1052 'Western Viceroy' and 'Peak' No D146 (later to become No 46009) sporting Brunswick- green livery.

(Bottom Right) : The 'Westerns' were ideally suited to work stone trains out of the Mendip quarries and No D1058 'Western Nobleman' is seen on 3rd September 1976 passing along the new arrival line at the Yeoman sidings at Merehead.   (All Hugh Ballantyne)

'WHISTLING WONDERS' - Class 20 Golden Jubilee

June 1957

The first of an initial order of 20 locomotives, D8000, was officially handed over to British Rail on 3rd June 1957 and was recorded arriving at Willesden on 19th June 1957, en route to an exhibition at Battersea Wharf. The new locomotives were designated 'Type 1' and the design was fairly unconventional, even at a time when steam engines were still being built. They were intended for freight traffic and no steam heating capability was fitted, although a through steam pipe was provided.

Between 1957 and 1968 a total of 228 Class 20s were built; 135 at the Vulcan Foundry and 93 at Robert Stephenson & Hawthorn, Darlington, delivered in green livery without yellow ends. The first 128 were built with a disc style train reporting system, while other locos carried four-character alpha/numeric equipment. Locos built for Scotland were fitted with space for token exchange apparatus. The depot allocations on first delivery were as follows:

D8000 - D8019	1D	Bow, Devon's Road	D8020	14B	Kentish Town
D8021 - D8027	34B	Hornsey	D8028 - D8030	64H	Leith Central
D8031	64C	Dalry Road	D8032 - D8034	60A	Inverness
D8035 - D8044	32A	Norwich	D8045 - D8049	34B	Hornsey
D8050 - D8069	41A	Darnall	D8070 - D8115	65A	Eastfield
D8116 - D8127	66A	Polmadie	D8128 - D8133	41A	Darnall
D8134 - D8136	2F	Bescot	D8137 - D8143	D02	LM Birmingham Div.
D8144 - D8199	D16	LM Nottingham Division	D8300 - D8309	50A	York
D8310 - D8313	51L	Thornaby	D8316 - D8327	64B	Haymarket

During the 1980s, the allocation was concentrated on just five maintenance depots: Bescot, Eastfield, Immingham, Tinsley and Toton and by 2000 all the class had been withdrawn from scheduled freight traffic, save for those members of the class reprieved by Direct Rail Services for use on nuclear flask trains, based at Carlisle Kingmoor TMD. These locomotives were refurbished and re-numbered:

1995 - 1996	Brush Traction, Loughborough	Nos. 20301 - 20305
1997 - 1998	RFS, Doncaster	Nos. 20306 - 20315

The class have alway been popular with enthusiasts, working summer-dated holiday trains to Skegness and on railtours; two notable tours being The Class 20 Locomotive Society's 'Three To The Sea' followed in the autumn of 1999, when three of the by then DRS owned Class 20/9s were used to power the 'Kosovo Train for Life' charter from the UK through to Kosovo, a trip which took a staggering two weeks to complete, but saw Class 20s operate under their own power through eastern Europe.

(Above) : A truly classic scene of Class 20s at work in the Leicestershire coalfield as Nos 20016 + 20196 head a loaded coal train off the Rawdon Colliery branch onto the Coalville line on 27th August 1981, while a light engine Class 47 waits for permission to proceed. The lines to the right lead to Donisthorpe and Measham collieries.

(Bottom left) : Railfreight Grey-liveried No 20023 double-heads No.20025 away from Norwich Thorpe on 11th July 1985 with a 'Speedlink' for Whitemoor Yard, which includes three bitumen TTAs and two household coal HEAs.

(Below) : Returning from the seaside on 17th August 1985, Nos 20157 + 20121 depart from Nottingham with the 15:25 (SO) Skegness - Leicester. (All Hugh Ballantyne)

Class 31 Golden Jubilee

October 1957

Fifty years ago this autumn, following the Type 1 (Class 20s), the second of the pilot diesel scheme appeared, when D5500 performed a main line test run from Derby to Chinley and back. After a repaint into Brunswick Green livery with two light grey bands, the loco was handed over to Stratford TMD at a ceremony at Loughborough on 31st October 1957. In fact, during the early years, the Class was almost exclusive to the Eastern Region and the first batch were nicknamed 'Toffee Apples' because of the bulbous shape of their control handles.

A total of 263 Class 31s were built at Brush Traction, Loughborough, between 1957 - 1962; traction provided by a Mirrlees JVS12T engine developing 1,250hp, and the locomotives mounted on a A1A - A1A wheel arrangement - unlike the 'Westerns', only the outer axles of each bogie were powered and the centre wheels were smaller in diameter than the outer ones.

(Above) : A panoramic view of Doncaster, prior to electrification of the ECML, and No 31248 leaving the sidngs on 23rd April 1981 with a good old fashoined goods train - 'The Plant' dominates the background.

(Top left) : Before re-numbering under TOPS, No 5822 (31290) stands at Sheffield Midland station on 14th June 1973 with a short parcels train, sporting a 4E11 reporting number - correctly displayed?

(Bottom Left) : What a busy scene - the market town of Skipton on 28th May 1975. No 31111 pulls away on a goods train, Class 47/0 No. 47270 stands in the station with the 08:00 St. Pancras - Glasgow and Class 45 No 45007 heads a ballast train in the opposite direction into the station. Those Class 31s not fitted with an indicator panel on top of the cab were christened 'Skinheads' by rail enthusiasts!

(Below) : Luton is the setting for No 31424, a member of the class equipped with Electric Train Supply, passing through the station on 1st August 1975 with an 'Up' engineers train. The scene is dominated by a magnificent semaphore gantry, beyond which is Luton North signalbox.   (All Hugh Ballantyne)

(Above) : Moving on to the Western Region, a grubby looking No 31416 approaches Westbury on 19th August 1978 with the 11:15 Britistol Temple Meads - Portsmouth Harbour, passing a long rake of loaded stone hoppers in the process. Note, the presence of semaphore signals; shortly after this photograph was taken, Westbury went over to Multiple Aspect Colour Signalling. (Hugh Ballantyne)

In 1964, when some of the Mirrlees JVS12T engines were given classified overhaul, major problems were identified and it was decided that to re-engine would be the most cost & time effective answer. Therefore, a batch of English Electric 12SVT units with an output of 1,470hp were ordered and fitted under a three year modernisation exchange programme.

Under the numerical classification, locomotives fitted with the original power units were classified 30, while those re-engined became Class 31. This class was in turn broken up into sub classes:

Class 31/0	: Original batch of locos.	
Class 31/1	: Original build	Nos 31101 - 31327
Class 31/4	: Modified 31/1s	Nos 31400 - 31469
	Fitted with Electric Train Supply	
Class 31/5	: Modified 31/4s	Nos 31500 - 31569
	Electric Train Supply isolated	
Class 31/6	: Modified 31/1s	Nos 31601 & 31602
	Electric Train Supply through wired for 'Push/Pull' operation	

The mixed traffic Class 31s have always found work on passenger duties and during the 1970s and '80s, they could be found throughout England & Wales, becoming synonymous with certain trains like the Birmingham - Norwich cross country trains, where they were staple motive power until displaced by 'Sprinters' in 1988. Today, the Class are still active on the main line, albeit in depleted numbers. Four locos. (Nos 31105 / 233 / 285 / 602) carry Network Rail yellow livery working the Company's gauging train. Furthermore, from July 2007, Nos 31452 and 31454 begin working Minehead - Bristol trains in connection with Butlins holiday traffic .....

.... long may they continue to see service!

LOCOMOTIVE NAMINGS

Notable namings this year involve members of the First GBRf Class 66/7 locomotive fleet:

26th January

At London's Euston station, five 'Metronet' Class 66/7s are named in a mass ceremony:

66718 'Gwyneth Dunwoody'
66719 'Metro-Land'
66720 'Metronet pathfinder'
66721 'Harry beck'
66722 'Sir Edward Watkin'

10th August

GBRf Managing Director, John Smith, a lifelong supporter of Sunderland AFC, achieves his ambition, when one of his locomotives is named after his team by the club's chairman, Niall Quinn:

66725 'Sunderland'

Interestingly, the design of the nameplate is identical to that carried by former LNER steam locomotives of the 'B17' 4-6-0 class; some of the 73-strong fleet being named after English football clubs.

(Above) : Gwyneth Dunwoody, the longest serving female Member of Parliament, Labour member for Crewe & Nantwich and chair of the Transport Sub Committee, names Metronet No 66719 'Gwyneth Dunwoody' at Euston station, alongside Andrew Lezala, Metronet Chief Executive. (Paul Biggs)

(Below) : Nameplate and number of 66725 'Sunderland'. (Carl Gorse)

(Bottom) : The newly named No 66725 'Sunderland' passes through Hartlepool on 14th September, hauling a rake of loaded HYA coal hoppers, forming 6H93, the 06:51 Tyne Dock - Drax. (Carl Gorse)

CARLISLE KINGMOOR OPEN-DAY

On Saturday, 7th July, Direct Rail Services hold their bi-annual open day at Carlisle Kingmoor Depot which attracts customers, members of staff and 1,000 lucky ticket-holders. By all accounts the event is a great success, during which DRS unveil its first DRS charter train of freshly painted Mark 3 carriages.

Also on display are ex-Freightliner Class 57 No 57011 repainted in DRS Compass livery along with DRS locos No 47501 and 47802, the latter displaying a light blue background to its Direct Rail Services lettering.

(Above) : A line up of sparkingly clean DRS locomotives at Kingmoor: Nos 57011 / 20311 / 37688 / 47802.

(Top Left) : To round off the day, DRS perform two naming ceremonies - No. 37688 is dedicated 'Kingmoor TMD' following refurbishment at Loughborough along with No 20311, named 'Class 20 Fifty' to commemorate 50 years of Type 1 operations. This close up view shows the nameplate applied to No 37688.

(Bottom Left) : The DRS charter train makes its debut on the day with a return trip to Tyneside. 'Eddie The Engine' No 66411 double-heads No 66405 and the DRS charter carriages on the return leg, running as 1Z67, the 16:25 Newcastle - Carlisle, seen passing under the architectural delight of Hexham signalbox.

(Below) : Meanwhile, a view inside Kingmoor TMD and three Classes of DRS traction receiving maintenance: from left to right, Nos 37038 / 37608 / 20310 / 66415. (All Carl Gorse)

BARROW HILL
TWENTY '20s' GALA

The Barrow Hill Roundhouse Diesel Gala this year will celebrate 50 years of the Class 20 locomotive by gathering as many 20s together as possible.

The event also includes two special trains running from the platform in the Roundhouse complex to the LaFarge Cement Works in Hope, on both Saturday and Sunday.

The format for the mainline shuttles is two DRS Class 20s top 'n' tailing two HNRC 20s.

(Above) : The original Type 1, No D8000 + No 20001 depart Barrow Hill Yard heading for the branch on Saturday, 15th July, with an afternoon shuttle. (Paul Biggs)

(Top Left) : Harry Needle Railroad Company (HNRC) Class 20 Nos 20901 + 20905 top 'n' tail DRS Class 20 Nos 20315 + 20311 'Class 20 Fifty' as they haul one of the special trains through Slitting Mill, running as 1Z20, Barrow Hill - Earles Sidings on Saturday, 14th July. (Mick Tindall)

(Bottom Left) : On the following day, 15th July, the special trains are out running again. This time on the return journey, one of the specials (1Z40 Earles Sidings - Barrow Hill), is seen with the DRS duo leading through Chesterfield station on a damp and dismal day, complete with an appropriate headboard. (Paul Biggs)

(Below) : Railfreight-Grey liveried No 20227 inside Barrow Hill roundhouse. (Mick Tindall)

EMRPS 'Photo Shoot'

(Above) : In the week leading up to the 'Twenty 20s Gala', the East Midlands Railway Preservation Society (EMRPS) arrange a day/night photographic session at Barrow Hill on 12th July and two images from this event are included, which give an excellent feel to the good old days at the roundhouse. Outside, looking in, No 20227 is glimpsed through the window.

(Opposite) : No 20001 sits proudly on one of the turntable roads.

(Both Mick Tindall)

1Z20, Swindon - Preston
'Yo Ho Ho'

(Opposite) : The 'Specials' section actually kicks off in the last week of 2006 in the period between Christmas and New Year, when enthusiasts are keen to have a break from all the festivities. No 66551 passes Class 142 'Pacer' unit No 142043 at Rainford on 29th December 2006, while working the Hooton Long Siding - Kirkby leg of the above tour; Nos 37194 + 37229 are DIT on the rear. Other locos to feature on the tour include Nos 60030, 66120, 66210 and & 86614.   (Fred Kerr)

0Z86, Bescot - Long Marston

(Right) : Three Class 86s are taken for storage from Bescot to Long Marston on 16th January. The train of locomotives, running as 0Z86, was scheduled to start from Bescot at 06:30 and arrive at its destination at around 10:50, but it was some three hours late leaving. Here is No 66100 with the trio of Class 86s (Nos 86251 + 86231 + 86229) at Evesham station in drizzling rain and very poor light.   (Peter Tandy)

5Z59, Long Marston - Chaddesden

(Below) : XP64-liveried No 47853 'Rail Express' stands on the East Loop at Honeybourne on 23rd January with a train of 10 JXAs taken out of storage at Long Marston.   (Peter Tandy)

1Z31, Birmingham New Street - Preston   *'Lancashire Witch'*

(Above) : On 20th January, the 'Lancashire Witch' sets off from Birmingham bound for Preston and a circuitous route via Chesterfield - Aldwarke Jn - Calder Bridge Jn - Greetland Jn and Copy Pit headed by Nos 31128 'Charybdis' and 31454 'The Heart of Wessex'; the 'Goyles' are seen passing Willington Footbridge.   (Paul Biggs)

6O87, Brierley Hill - Southampton Western Docks

(Below) : During February, several train loads of containerised scrap move from Brierley Hill in the West Midlands to Southampton for export, thought to be destined for China! The front portion of the initial service is seen here on St. Valentine's Day being shunted by No 66187 at Brierley Hilll prior to departure.   (Don Gatehouse)

1Z47, Crewe - Llandrindod Wells   *'Welsh Central Liner II'*

(Above) : Classic traction, in the shape of Class 40 No 40145, approaching Ashchurch with a Pathfinder tour from Crewe to Llandrindod Wells on Saturday, 3rd March 2007.   (Peter Tandy)

1Z56, York - Holyhead   *'Tubular Belle'*

(Page 100, overleaf) : Excellent timing; just as a Midland Mainline HST decides to pass in the opposite direction, Class 45/1 No 45112 'Royal Army Ordnance Corps' is captured perfectly as she approaches the cameraman at Clay Cross (09:34hrs) at the head of this 'Peak Farewell' merrymaker tour to Holyhead on 7th January. The 'Peak' is scheduled for withdrawal due to the prohibitive cost of OTMR fitment and will be a sad loss!   (Nigel Gibbs)

1Z52, London Waterloo - Okehampton   *'Western South Western'*

(Page 101) : Classic location, classic traction .... Class 52 No 1015 'Western Champion' running in the guise of No 1046 'Western Marquis' on one side only passes Eastleigh on 24th February with the 'Western South Western'. The train is making its way to Salisbury where it will then proceed down the ex-London & South Western Railway route to Exeter and thence via Crediton to Okehampton.   (Nigel Gibbs)

SPECIALS

5Z47, Derby - Bishops Lydeard

(Above) : Class 47/4 locomotives Nos 47847 and 47839 'Pegasus' are rostered to complete a coaching stock move from Boness in Scotland to Bishops Lydeard on the West Somerset Railway in connection with a forthcoming Gala weekend. The pair work south from Derby on 10th March and are pictured passing Bromsgrove with a rake of all maroon coaches, viz: 4831, 4836, 1730, 4856, 13230, 35185, 13229, 3115, 1859 and 3096.   (Don Gatehouse)

5Z18, Wolverton - Selhurst

(Below) : A splash of green and two contrasting shades. A refurbished Class 456 EMU, sporting Southern livery of white & dark green with light green semi-circles at one end of each vehicle, sits between two barrier vehicles, hauled by Freightliner's No 47816 in ex-First Great Western green livery. The ensemble is approaching Milton Keynes on 13th March, running as 5Z18, the 11:13 Wolverton - Selhurst.   (Nigel Gibbs)

CHELTENHAM RACE SPECIALS

(Below) : Cheltenham Race Week generally produces some additional loco-hauled trains and this year is no exception. Class 67s No 67021+ 67029 perform on the London Euston - Cheltenham race specials all week (Tuesday, 13th March to Friday, 16th March) and the pair are seen on the first day passing Dogbirdge. It just shows how how little work there is for the Class 67, if the same locomotives can be dedicated to a train for four consecutive days!

(Bottom) : Apart from a few steel trains to Round Oak, the section of line between Worcester and Abbotswood Junction Junction sees little loco-hauled activity and fortunately the 1T66, Birmingham New Street - Cheltenham is routed this way. Here, on Friday, 16th March, No 57601 passes the lower quadrant bracket signal at Norton Junction, where the Cheltenham line diverges from the Cotswold Line to Oxford.   (Both Peter Tandy)

1Z20, Crewe - Ipswich

'Twenty/Twenty Vision'

A pleasant surprise for passengers awaiting the 05:30hrs start from Crewe on 10th March - not two DRS Class 20s, but three! Someone in DRS decide three locos are needed to take the train to East Anglia - Nos 20313 + 20315 plus No 20314 thrown in for good measure. The tour visits Ely and the East Suffolk Line, including a trip down the branch to Sizewell (BNFL).

(Above) : On the outward journey, the trio pass Whitemoor Fen on the approach to March.   (Nigel Gibbs)

(Below) : After the scheduled stop at Saxmundham, Nos 20313/ 314 and 315 storm along the single track section at Wickham Market with 1Z21, Ipswich Yard - Cambridge Yard via Sizewell.   (James Welham)

CELEBRATING IN STYLE

Luxury Charters

1Z94, London Victoria - Cardiff

(Above) : I know, just another image of EWS celebrity Class 67 No 67029 hauling the VSOE, but it's my first view of the 'Skip'. The occasion is the Wales v England rugby union international at the Millennium Staduim on 17th March and passengers 'wine & dine' as the train passes Highworth Junction, just under a mile to the east of Swindon station. After the photograph, back home for some lunch and watch the Six Nations Rugby Championship on television and for Wales to record their only victory of the campaign. (Martin Buck)

VSOE, London Victoria - Paddock Wood

(Page 106, overleaf) : This delightful composition has all the attributes; attractive location, superb colour and a fine balance of light & shade! Good food on a great train - is there a better way to spend Mothering Sunday? No 67021 is on the front of the VSOE Pullman stock with the distinctively liveried No 67029 on the rear, seen approaching Leigh station near Tonbridge on 18th March. The train proceeds to Paddock Wood before returning to Victoria later in the day. (Alan Hazelden)

1Z82, London Waterloo - New Milton

(Page 107) : GBRf Class 73 locomotives No 73208 'Kirsten' and 73206 'Lisa' are paired up to work a special 'Wedding Belle' private charter on 16th March using the luxurious 'Queen of Scots' rake of heritage coaching stock. The train is seen on the outward journey at 12:47hrs passing Battledown Farm on the outskirts of Basingstoke. The flyover is part of Worting Junction and carries the 'Up Southampton Main line   . (Ian Ball)

86101 'Sir William A Stanier FRS'

Due to the stirling efforts of the AC Locomotive Group, Class 86/2 No 86101 'Sir William A. Stanier FRS' makes a welcome return to the mainline. The charter detailed below, run in association with Victa Railfreight, hoped (and advertised) to use Freightliner Class 47 No 47150 in what would have almost certainly been its last ever passenger run before scheduled withdrawal at the end of the month, but this did not happen.

1Z43, Carlisle - Holyhead   *'Ynys Mon Express'*

(Above) : On 24th March, No 86101 is seen passing Euxton Junction on the WCML whilst working 1Z43, the 06:33 Carlisle - Holyhead Compass / Victa Railfreight charter as far as Crewe, from where Class 47/8s No. 47812 + No 47815 'Great Western' work the Crewe - Holyhead - Crewe leg in top 'n' tail formation.   (Fred Kerr)

(Below) : Back at Carlisle in the evening, No 86101 complete with headboard is atop No 47815 (D1748) and poses for a night-time exposure for the assembled cameramen.   (Carl Gorse)

'ROVERS'
UP FOR THE CUP

1Z47, Doncaster - Cardiff

(Right) : On April Fools Day, Doncaster Rovers win the Johnstone's Paint Trophy at the Millennium Stadium, Cardiff, by beating Bristol Rovers 3-2 after extra time. Some of the supporters travel to the match by special train, and one hauled by No 67005 'Queens Messenger', is seen passing Kingsbury. All the coaches (except one) are air-conditioned Mark 2 in design and display Virgin, Arriva and ex-InterCity livery.   (Paul Biggs)

ARMED ESCORT

5Z76, Carlisle Kingmoor - Keyham

(Above) : DRS Class 66/4 locomotives have no mandatory freight turns in the south west of England, so it is a real bonus on Wednesday, 28th March, when not one, but two locomotives appear! Nos 66408 and 66406 provide a contrast of colour against the backdrop of Red Sandstone cliffs as they pass Coryton Cove hauling 5Z76, the 19:08 Carlisle Kingmoor – Keyham formed of two Mark 2 coaches Nos 9428 and 9419. The two coaches are the DRS armed escort coaches used on nuclear flask workings and are en-route to Devonport Dockyard near Keyham in readiness for the following nights flask move to Sellafield.   (Robert Sherwood)

SPECIALS

2Z69, Hitchin - Peterborough

(Below) : On 21st March, Network rail organise an outing around Cambridgeshire for the benefit of stakeholders to show off its plans for Peterborough station and the upgrade of the line between Hitchin and Cambridge. In fact, we feature the latter line here with 2Z69, the 10:10 departure ex-Hitchin, passing Litlington on the approach to Royston with No 47853 'Rail Express' leading and large-logo No 47847 DIT bringing up the rear. The train is making its way to Peterborough via Cambridge and Ely.						(Nigel Gibbs)

4Z66, Chaddesden - Purfleet

(Above) : On 11th April, No. 66419 passes Oakley on the Midland Mainline with 4Z66, formed of empty KAA wagons bound for Purfleet in readiness of the new Ditton/Grangemouth Victa Westlink intermodals. (Nigel Gibbs)

1Z37, Birmingham International - Onllwyn   *'Principality Freighter'*

(Above) : This charter epitomises what a railtour is all about - good traction and a good selection of 'freight only' lines. On 14th April, the 'Principality Freighter' features two Class 37'4s, a Class 60 plus visits to the Swansea District Line, Onllwyn, Cwmgwrach and Uskmouth. As the 37s (out of view) head for Onllwyn, No 60038 'Avestapolarit' trails the train at Neath & Brecon Junction in readiness to work the train back to the junction, where the 37s will take over for the trip to Cwmgwrach.

(Below) : For the return journey, the reporting code changes to1Z74 and the two 37s (No 37422 'Cardiff Canton' + No. 37410) make a stirring sight as they power through Bridgend.   (Both James Welham)

CARGO-D

A new fleet of 17 refurbished coaches in BR corporate blue / grey livery enters the charter market, all but one being Mk 3s, initiated by operator Cargo-D; a railway organisation specialising in 3rd party solutions for freight, passenger and locomotive and wagon provision. The vehicles will be made available for charter, corporate and specialist TOC work, which can be complemented by Mk 3 catering vehicles, sleeper carriage and a Mk 2e BSO brake coach.

The Cargo-D fleet is:	Mk 3a RFM	-	10202 / 102046
	Mk 3b FO	-	11065 / 071 / 083 / 084 / 086 / 089 / 097
	Mk 3a TSO	-	12014 / 038 / 043 / 053 / 119
	Mk 3b DVT	-	82117
	Mk 3 SLEP	-	10588
	Mk 2e BSO	-	9508

The Cargo-D carriages are maintained alongside the already extensive contingent of Mk 2 and Mk 1 vehicles at Crewe, which LNWR look after on behalf of loco-hauled coaching stock operators. LNWR, Crewe, is responsible for the fleet management, repair and maintenance of the coaches and Cargo-D is located at the rail-connected ex-military base at Long Marston in Warwickshire.

1Z47, Blackburn - Great Yarmouth   *'Eastern Fellsman'*

(Top Left) : Resplendent in two-tone green livery, No 47815 'Great Western' powers through March on 5th May with the return 'Eastern Fellsman' charter, running as 1Z48 , the 05:10 Great Yarmouth - Blackburn and No 47847 DIT on the rear. The stock is the new rake of Mark 3 coaches owned by Cargo-D.   (James Welham)

5Z63, Carnforth - Barnetby

(Above) : The Little North Western route between Carnforth and Settle Junction sees little loco-hauled activity and an even smaller amount makes its way onto the pages of railway periodicals. In driving rain, No 47826 'Springburn' pilots Gresley 4-6-2 Pacific No 60009 'Union of South Africa' past Wennington on 18th May with 5Z63, the Carnforth - Barnetby ECS for the following day's 'Hadrian' tour from Cleethorpes to Morpeth.   (Andrew Naylor)

1Z21, Mills Hill - Ely   **'Fenland Cathedral & Sunrise Coast Explorer'**

(Bottom Left) : A striking composition, if not a hair-raising experience for the photographer! This Green Express tour passes Lolham, near Peterborough on 21st April with two-tone green No D1648 (47851 'Traction Magazine') heading the tour and, for those wondering, Mills Hill is on the Manchester Victoria - Rochdale main line. (John Rudd)

1Z55, Bristol Temple Meads - Whitby

(Above) : Cotswold Rail locomotives No 47810 'Captain Sensible' and No 47813 'Joe Strummer' work this Heartland Rail merrymaker excursion to Whitby on 12th May, running in top 'n' tail formation along the scenic Esk Valley line. An elevated vantage point provides a panoramic view of the town of Whitby, situated on both sides of the River Esk, with the famous abbey and St. Mary's church dominating the skyline. The train is seen languishing in a siding prior to No 47810 leading the charter back to Bristol.   (Carl Gorse)

The RETURN of No. 12 'SARAH SIDDONS'

She returns to the main line for the first time since 2001. Metronet and London Underground celebrate the occasion by operating a special train featuring Metropolitan Railway electric No. 12 'Sarah Siddons' and the Class 20 Locomotive Society's Railfreight red-stripe Class 20 No 20227 and a rake of ex-BR 4-TC stock, Nos 76297 / 71163/ 70823 / 76324. 'Sarah Siddons' was one of 20, 65mph locos, built by Metroploitan-Vickers in 1921 and named after a famous 18th Century tragedy actress. The locomotive was overhauled at Ruislip Depot by Technical Services and the Train Modification Depot.

(Below) : On the special day, 10th June, 'Sarah Siddons' leads special No 710 south through Northwood with No 20227 bringing up the rear, running from Amersham to Harrow-on-the-Hill.   (Ralf Edge)

CAMBRIAN ADVENTURES

1Z37, Cardiff Central - Pwllheli   *'Snowdonian'*

(Overleaf - Page 116) : What a view! Looking across Cardigan Bay towards the mountains of Snowdonia in the background, No 37410 heads 1Z37, the 06:00 Cardiff Central - Pwllheli railtour on 19th May past Criccieth promenade. The tour is worked from the ouset by Nos 37406 + 37410 until Machynlleth, where No 37410 proceeds on her own for the journey to Pwllheli and back.   (Richard Jones)

1Z40, The Cambrian Coast Express   *'Cambrian Coast Express'*

(Page 117) : Powering through Belle Vue in the outskirts of Shrewsbury, No 40145 heads 1Z40, the 06:05 Leeds - Aberystwyth on 2nd June, believed to be the first Class 40 to work on the Cambrian Line for 20 years. This prompted the author to have a look in his own records to see when he last made a visit to the Cambrian hauled by a Class 40 locomotive; only the two recorded runs listed below.   (Nigel Gibbs)

40009	22nd July 1984	1Z10,	Manchester Victoria - Aberystwyth
40106	4th December 1982	1L02,	Crewe - Aberystwyth

The latter, a special train taking shareholders to the Vale of Rheidol Annual General Meeting in Aberystwyth.

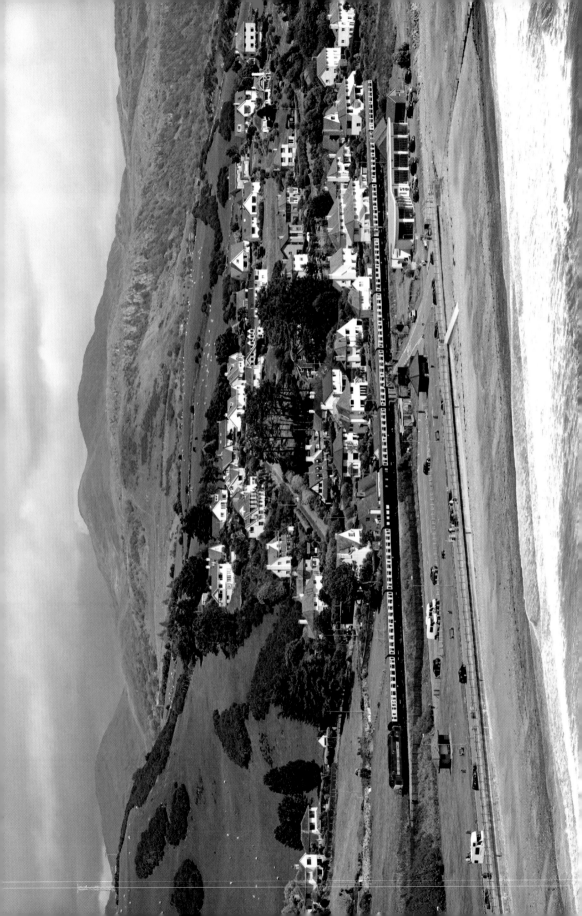

GLASTONBURY 'ROCKS'

(Top Left) : Commencing 20th June, Festival specials are laid on to take 'rockers' from Swindon / Taunton to Castle Cary for the annual musical extravaganza at Glastonbury. Four Class 67s are deployed on the shuttles with No 67006 'Royal Sovereign' paired with No 67015 and EWS Corporate-liveried No 67029 with No 67013. On the first day, No 67006 passes Berkeley Marsh heading 2Z55, Swindon - Castle Cary. (Nic Joynson)

'BUTLINS EXPRESS'

A new summer-dated loco-hauled service starts running this year to Minehead - notable because it is operated by Victa Westlink Rail, using top 'n' tail Class 31s from Mainline Rail, air-conditioned coaches, and will run throughout calling at all stations on the West Somerset Railway.

1Z35, 11:10 Minehead - Bristol Temple Meads

1Z39, 14:06 Bristol Temple Meads - Minehead

The services will run Monday, Friday, Saturday between 20th July - 27th August.

A second new service commences on 7th July between Bristol Temple Meads and Weymouth (2O67 outward and 2V67 return) using EWS Class 67s as motive power, but only lasts for four Saturdays. Apparently, EWS cannot operate passenger services under its Safety Case - just charter trains and specials. A knock-on effect of this ruling is that some loco-hauled additional services planned to run between Exeter St. Davids and Newton Abbot for the Dawlish Carnival may be cancelled.

(Bottom Left) : On Friday, 10th August, No 31454 'Pride of Wessex' and No 31452 'Minotaur' top 'n' tail 1Z39, the 14:06 Bristol TM – Minehead 'Butlins Express' , which is seen passing 40 Steps, following the train's scheduled Taunton station stop. (Robert Sherwood)

1Z20, Barrow Hill - Skegness   *'Jolly Fisherman'*

(Above) : Just like the good old days, when pairs of Class 20s could be seen working summer-dated holiday trains from the East Midlands to Skegness, running from Chesterfield, Derby and Leicester. Well, such 'Merrymaker' style trips make a return as we see here with DRS Class 20/3 locomotive Nos 20311 + 20315 powering through Ancaster on 29th August with 1Z20, the 08:15 Barrow Hill - Skegness 'Jolly Fisherman'. (Nigel Gibbs)

A CHARITABLE OCCASION

The
Bristol Coal-Stone Haul

On 3rd June, Network Rail (Bristol) lay on a charter, in fact a series of mini-tours (1Z20 to 1Z27) in aid of the 'Railway Children' charity taking in some branch lines in the Bristol area. The Locomotives involved are Network Rail Class 31/1 Nos 31105 + 31285 and heritage Class 50 No 50049 'Defiance' and the tour visits Portbury, Hallen Marsh, Tytherington and Severn Beach.

The respective sections of the tour are made up as follows:

1Z20, Bristol Temple Meads - Portbury	1Z21, Portbury - Bath Spa
1Z22, Bath Spa - St Andrews Road	1Z24, St Andrews Road - Tytherington
1Z25, Tytherington - Bristol Temple Meads	1Z26, Bristol Temple Meads - Severn Beach
1Z27, Severn Beach - Bristol Temple Meads	

(Above) : The train is seen after arriving at Tytherington Quarry behind the 31s (with the 50 just out of view), becoming the first loco-hauled train into this location since February. In fact, it is 30 years ago, on 22nd October 1977, when Stratford based Nos 31005 + 31019 visited the branch with the RPPR Class 31/0 'Toffee Apple' Farewell tour - 1Z10, the 08:03 ex-London Paddington. The lack of a headcode box on No 31105 gives a similar Class 31/0 appearance. (Richard Giles)

(Below) : The two 'Goyles', complete with headboard, are seen powering 1Z22, Bath Spa - St. Andrew's Road through Oldfield Park, Bath, on the third leg of the 'Bristol Coal-Stone Haul.' (James Welham)

DRS - Training Runs on ECML

At Kingmoor Open Day on 7th July, DRS launches itself as a stand-alone charter operator using a rake of refurbished first class Mark 3 vehicles, which will be made available for hire. Prior to the introduction of Grand Central's new passenger services between Sunderland and London King's Cross, crew training runs take place using the DRS rake of Mark 3s and two DRS 47's.

(Above) : On 16 August, the special train from Sunderland is worked by No 47501 and No 47802 in top 'n' tail formation and is seen at Marholm, Peterborough, running neck and neck with Freightliner's No 66536 hauling 4Z79, Leeds - Felixstowe freightliner. (Alan Hazelden)

(Above) : On the previous day, No 47237 (No 47802 on rear) approaches London King's Cross platform 2 with 1Z43, the 09:06 ex-Sunderland and the first day the special train manages to reach King's Cross; terminating at Connington on the Monday and cancelled altogether on the Tuesday. (Nigel Gibbs)

40145 - A Question of Style

Call me old fashioned, but I am somewhat of a traditionalist and prefer classic traction to carry the livery as worn in BR days, especially when it involves a Class 40. You can decide for yourself ....

Home for the CFPS Class 40 is the East Lancashire Railway (ELR), which runs for some 8-miles linking Heywood - Bury Bolton St. - Ramsbottom - Rawtenstall. The locomotive is named 'East Lancashire Railway' at Bury on 25th July and the repaint, sponsored by DVD producers Visions International, is the result of a poll of CFPS members. No 'whistlers' ever carried this livery in BR service, although in 1991 this livery was previously carried by the loco and numbered 40445, gaining mock ETH boxes in the process.

(Above) : The CFPS Class 40 in Large-Logo livery with wrap round yellow cab ends is seen on the day of its naming with observation saloon No. W150266 passing Burrs on the East Lancashire Railway.   (Paul Biggs)

(Below) : This close up view shows the 'Whistler' in BR-Blue livery heading along the WCML at Grayrigg on 7th June + support coach + No 47145 'Myrddin Emrys', running under reporting code 5Z40.   (Andrew Naylor)

JUST CHAMPION!

1Z52, Ealing Broadway - Aberystwyth

'Alliance Cambrian Express'

History in the making, as the first Class 52 hauled passenger train reaches the 'Mid Wales' seaside resort of Aberystwyth, home to the University of Wales. The special train is sponsored by Pathfinder Tours, EWS, Riviera Trains and the Diesel Traction Group and is marketed as 'The Alliance Cambrian Coast Express'

(Above) : On the outward journey, No D1015 'Western Champion' crosses Clettwr Bridge, 1st September.

(Below) : Some 25-minutes after her arrival, D1015 runs round the stock in readiness for the booked 16:10hrs departure from Aberystwyth and the six hour journey back home. (Both Richard Jones)

VINTAGE TRAINS

Vintage Trains is one of the U.K.'s leading operators of main line steam train excursions, based in the Midlands, offering an attractive and varied choice of destinations, such as the popular 'Shakespeare Express' running on Sundays between Birmingham and Stratford-upon-Avon. As a subsidiary of the Birmingham Railway Museum Trust, ticket sales income is reinvested in running, maintaining and rebuilding historic engines, rolling stock and equipment kept at their home base - Tyseley Locomotive Works.

New for 2007 - Vintage Trains introduce their 'Explorer' trains, which will be hauled by classic diesel locomotives to a choice of scenic routes and interesting destinations. It is planned to utilise a Heritage Class 50 as traction for this purpose.

Unfortunately, the Company make an inauspicious start on 12th May when Class 50 No 50049 'Defiance' fails shortly after Radlett (Milepost 13.25 to be exact!) with a coolant leak while working 1Z50, Tyseley - Havant 'Pompey Vectis Explorer' and the tour is curtailed; the train being rescued by No 47853 'Rail Express'.

1Z50, Tyseley - Eastbourne   *'Airborne Eastbourne'*

(Top Left) : Undaunted by their earlier setback, Vintage Trains try again on 18th August and No 50049 passes Oakley on the Midland Mainline (No 57601 at the rear for the return journey) taking passengers to the seafront airshow at Eastbourne. The train, operated by West Coast Railways, is a mix of vehicles, including three 'Pullman' cars in a formation of 9496 + 99349 + 99361 + 99353 + 3309 + 3351 + 1201 + 5928.   (Nigel Gibbs)

WHAT A LOT!

1Z57, Kensington Olympia - Chester

(Above) : This special train is the result of a prize in a Railway Children charity auction, won by Stagecoach, taking invited corporate guests to Chester .... very nice too! On 14th September, No 57315 'The Mole' approaches Didcot North Junction on the outward leg hauling the 'Queen of Scots' trainset, which consists a number of styles of heritage coaching stock in a mixture of understated liveries, contratsting markedly with the immaculately presented but guadily coloured 'Mole'. Sister locomotive No 57316 'Fab 1' brings up the rear.   (Alan Hazelden)

THE RETURN of R.S.G.

(Bottom Left) : After a 12-month break, Martin Walker's Deltic No 55022 'Royal Scots Grey' returns to the main line for the first time on 21st September, hauling Heritage traction, Nos D5310, D8020, 37175 and 40145, from Bury to Bo'ness. On 5th October, she turns out on 1Z50, the 07:20 King's Cross - Inverness 'Autumn Highlander' charter and is seen heading along the ECML at Kempsford. No 50049 'Defiance' is DIT on the rear, which will also feature on the tour along with No 40145.   (Nigel Gibbs)

RHTTs - DRS Style

Autumn sees the arrival of the annual programme of Railhead Treatment Trains (Water Cannon / Leafbusters', etc) across the network and this year the subject of illustration is DRS, especially with the introduction of their newly acquired Class 57s on the Anglia RHTTs for the first time. Unfortunately, the 57s do not cover themselves in glory and suffer several failures.

(Above) : No 57011 top 'n' tails No 57009 on 17th October passing over Cattawade Viaduct, Manningtree, with 3S60, the 09:20 Stowmarket - Shenfield Water Cannon; terminating at Colchester due to late running. (Andy Small)

(Below) : Two days later, the ensemble trundles through Hatfield Peverel with 3S60 running main line all the way between Stowmarket and Shenfield. In total, there are four RHTTs covering Anglia, all based at Stowmarket, taking in Southend, Clacton, Harwich, Lowestoft, Cromer, Ely, Cambridge and Braintree. (James Welham)

(Above) : The first time a DRS Class 37 is used on a Great Eastern RHTT occurs on 18th October when No 37038 steps in to fill the breach following the failure of No 57011, seen passing Ingatestone with 3S60, the 09:20 Stowmarket - Shenfield Goods Loop RHTT with No 57009 on the rear. (James Welham)

(Below) : Meanwhile, this superb composition depicts Nos 20304 and 20305 standing in the 'Down Station Siding', Sheffield, a tadge before 19:37hrs on 5th October with 3S11, the 15:48 York - Chesterfield RHTT. The image is obtained by an exposure of 2.0s, f8 aperture, ISO 200 and a 53mm focal length. (Ralf Edge)

(Above) : The RHTTs working in Scotland involve Jarvis providing four MPVs, based at Shettleston, Slateford and two sets at Kilmarnock, plus DRS providing the traction for the Inverness based train. On the Highland Line, No 66429 brings up the rear (No 66423 leading) of 3S95, Inverness - Inverness RHTT on 23rd October passing Murthly, south of Dunkeld. The train makes a circular trip via Aberdeen, Dundee and Perth.

(Below) : As an unidentified Class 170 unit comes off the Tay Bridge forming an Edinburgh - Aberdeen service, Nos 66402 + 66408 leave Dundee and make their way to Perth with 3S95 on 13th October; the train is double-headed on this occasion due to a booked loco change at Perth. *(Both Jim Ramsay)*

E.P.S. 37s FAREWELL

1Z87, London Euston - Folkestone Harbour

'Atomic Harbour Master'

Pathfinder's 'Atomic Harbour Master' on Saturday, 20th October, offers enthusiasts a final chance to experience haulage behind EUKL's Class 37/6s, prior to the fleet becoming redundant at the end of the year. After No 86101 'Sir William A Stanier' brings the tour into London Euston from Crewe (1Z86) Nos 37601 + 37603 visit the Folkestone Harbour and Dungeness branches, before returning as far as Willesden.

(Above) : The pair (37603 nearest camera) are shown attacking the 1 in 30 climb away from the Harbour with the first part of the return leg 1Z88, the 14:00 to Dungeness. By this point the tour was running an hour late - still well within RST (Railtour Standard Time)!

(Marc Ely)

(Below) : In glorious autumn sunshine, after visiting Folkestone Harbour, the tour proceeds to Dungeness and on the approach to Dungeness Power station, the 37s trundle along the branch towards the Network Rail limit with No 37601 leading this particular leg.

(James Welham)

HERITAGE

Setting the Scene ....

The lure of 'Classic' diesel traction ......

Rail enthusiasts in their thousands flock to the many preserved railway lines around the country to enjoy the sight & sound of old diesels at close quarters and this section provides a flavour of what's on offer with a small selection of photographs.

Nowadays, preservation comes under the all-encompassing 'Heritage' banner and most of the preserved lines actively covet the enthusiast by laying on special events, such as regular timetabled workings, diesel 'Galas' and 'Photo Shoots' - in fact, something for everyone.

Great Central Railway

(Above) : The Great Central Railway runs for 8 miles from Loughborough Central to Leicester North and with double track this gives the GCR a 'Mainline' image. Class 47 No D1705 'Sparrowhawk' sits at Loughborough Central station on a goods train during a night shoot on 9th March.   (Mick Tindall)

(Top Right) : An idyllic setting for No D5401, probably better known to readers as 'Push Pull' Class 27/1 No 27112, passing Woodthorpe, near Loughboroughton, in a patch of sun on 23rd March with 2B25, the 16:10 Leicester North - Loughborough Central, or should it be 2B17?

(Bottom Right) : Many private railways have enough rolling stock to form representative demonstration freight trains and the Great Central is one of the leading exponents. On 4th September, D5401 is seen again, but this time sporting a half-yellow warning panel, posing for the camera at at Kinchley Lane, during an EMRPS photographic charter using the Windcutter wagons.   (Both Paul Biggs)

Churnet Valley

(Above) : Class 37/0 No 37075 pilots a Class 104 DMU away from Leekbrook on 1st June on the occasion of the Churnet Valley's diesel gala. The 37, fitted with snowploughs, was purchased for preservation in 1999 and now belongs to the 5C Loco Group. This heritage railway is situated in the heart of the Staffordshire moorlands and offers a 6.5-mile return journey from Cheddleton station (near Leek) to the hamlet of Consall Forge.   (Paul Biggs)

Colne Valley Railway

(Below) : EWS-liveried Class 31/1 No 31255 awaits departure time at Castle Hedingham station on 8th April with a short rake of 'blood & custard' Mark 1 coaches. This is a completely reconstructed country station and railway within sight of a 12th century castle, albeit with only a 1-mile length of track on which to operate. (James Welham)

Midland Railway Centre

The Centre is preservation with a difference; a massive 57 acre museum site and 35 acre country park enabling the Centre to offer 'More than just a railway.' A seven-road Matthew Kirtley Museum allows much of the collection to be on display and for most of the locomotives to be stored under cover. The site boasts 3.5 miles of standard guage line complete with Midland signals, restored signalboxes, Butterley station, plus the scenic delights of Butterley Reservoir and Golden Valley.

The preserved line also has the benefit of having access to the main line at Codnor Park Junction.

(Above) : Class 50 No. 50007 'Sir Edward Elgar' enters Swanwick Junction station on 23rd June with the 10:00 Butterley - Riddings, this being the first service of the day at the CFA Gala. Readers may recall the general disquiet when No 50007 'Hercules' was accordingly repainted and renamed in the 1980s.   (Paul Biggs)

Overleaf:

(Page 134) :

This evocative image was taken during an EMPRS photo shoot on 3rd February and is reminiscent of former BR days in the late 1950s / early 1960s with a locomotive sporting Brunswick green livery, half-yellow warning panel, hauling a rake of vacuum brake, steam heated Mark 1 coaches. Class 40 No D212 'Aureol' pauses at Swanwick station for the benefit of assembled cameras.   (Mick Tindall)

'Chopperfest'

On 19th May, a special diesel gala takes place to celebrate 50 years of the Type 1, Class 20 locomotive, and is the first such event of the year. The event takes place at Butterley with eight Class 20s in action:

D8007	D8132	D8154
20001	20189	20227
20303	20404	

(Page 135) : MASSIVE! Well, that's how the photographer describes this particular occasion.

Nos 20303 / 20304 / 20001 / 20189 and 20227 power the last run of the day from Riddings to Hammersmith, seen here passing Golden Valley - thanks going to the driver for stopping the train 150 yards in front of the waiting cameramen until the sun came out!   (Mick Tindall)

Nottingham Transport Heritage Centre

(Below) : The Nottingham Transport Heritage Centre is home to the preserved Great Central Railway in Nottinghamshire, based in Ruddington alongside Rushcliffe Country Park. The ex-GCR line is still in situ. from Loughborough South Junction, which enables access to the British Gypsum plant at Hotchley Hill, East Leake. A panoramic view shows Ruddington yard on 26th August and Class 47/0 No 47292 running in preservation for the first time, hauling a rake of ex-Gatwick Express stock.   (Paul Biggs)

Battlefield Steam Railway

(Below) : The Battlefield Steam Railway has its headquarters in Shackerstone station, near Market Bosworth, Leicestershire and runs for 4.75 miles linking Shackerstone - Market Bosworth - Shenton. On 16th September, two Class 31/1s No. 31130 'Calder Hall Power Station' + No 31101 in Bescot pet colours, approaches Market Bosworth on 16th September - one month prior to the Class 31's 50th anniversary.   (Paul Biggs)

Mid-Norfolk Railway

(Below) : The date is 16th March and represents when the Stratford 47 Group's Class 47/4 No 47596 makes its inaugural run in preservation - in fact, five out & back trips along the Mid Norfolk Railway during the day. The locomotive, in revised blue livery, leaves Dereham station on its first run, the 09:00 to Wymondham passing two excellent examples of semaphore signals. The Mid-Norfolk Railway is operational between Dereham and Wymondham, and the long-term aim is to reach Fakenham. (Paul Biggs)

South Devon Railway - 'The Primrose Line'

(Below) : The line runs for 7 miles between Totnes and Buckfastleigh beside the beautiful River Dart, where we see Class 37/3 No 37321 'Loch Treig' on 29th March pulling away from a signal check at Hood Bridge with 5Z21, Buckfastleigh – Bishops Bridge ECS. The 37 is probably better known to readers when named 'Gartcosh', alloctaed to Motherwell, and could be found working Hunterston - Ravenscraig iron ore trains. (Robert Sherwood)

Nene Valley Railway

The Nene Valley runs for 7.5 miles from Wansford to Peterborough and its unique collection includes locomotives and coaches from 10 countries and two continents. For this reason, it is a regular location for TV and film makers, such as 'Goldeneye', for example, where the Cambridgeshire countryside doubles for locations like Russia!

(Above) : During a night shoot on 24th February, Large Logo Class 56 No 56057 'British Fuels' is stabled alongside Class 33/0 No 33065 'Sealion' outside the old steam shed at Wansford. (Mick Tindall)

(Centre) : A 'Diesel Gala' takes place during the first weekend of March and a selection of four images are included to mark the event.

A right teddy bear's picnic and three for the price of one! Class 14 Nos D9516 + D9520 + D9523 hurtle towards Castor Cutting, between Orton Mere and Wansford, with a service from Peterborough. (James Welham)

(Left) : No 33065 'Sealion' and Class 31/1 No 31271 'Stratford 1840 - 2001' double-head a special working near Castor with the 'Crompton' producing plenty of clag! (Paul Biggs)

(Above) : Class 40 No 306 'Atlantic Conveyor' passes the signal at Sutton Cross on 3rd March. The loco was named 'Atlantic Conveyor' to commemorate the 14,950 tonne 'roll on - roll off' Cunard container ship, which was sunk by two Exocet missiles during the 1982 Falklands War.

(Below) : Paying a visit to the Nene Valley, Class 66/7 No. 66718 'Gwyneth Dunwoody' nears Castor with a rake of continental coaches, forming the 12:15 Wansford - Peterborough.   (Both Paul Biggs)

North Yorkshire Moors Railway

What can one say about this railway? Being one of the most popular in the UK, it is also, with 18 miles of track between Grosmont and Pickering, one of the longest of preserved lines. As with other preserved lines, 'Diesel Galas' are not only a huge attraction for enthusiasts, but a great revenue earner for the owners. A gala takes place over the weekend of 20th - 22nd April and a selection of images from the event are illustrated here.

(Above) : The original Class 37, No D6700, is passed by Class 50 No 50027 'Lion' on the approach to Grosmont with a service from Pickering - quite a contrast in liveries!

(Below) : Meanwhile, 'Skinhead' Class 31/1 No 31108 in immaculate Railfreight grey livery passes through a heavily wooded section of the NYMR at Green End.

(Above) : The NYMR abounds in beautiful scenery and there are plenty of superb vantage points from which to capture the 'perfect shot'. Displaying a 2P77 reporting code, the CFPS Class 40 No 40145 passes through Water Ark with a Grosmont - Pickering service formed of seven blood & custard Mark 1 coaches.

(Below) : Deltic No D9009 'Alycidon' passes Darnholm with a service to Pickering.   (All Carl Gorse)

Peak Rail

In 1968, the railway between Matlock and Buxton through the Peak National Park was closed and lifted; once being the Midland Railway's main line between Manchester Central and London St.Pancras. In 1975 a group of enthusiasts formed the Peak Railway Society with the aim of re-opening the line, which now operates 4 miles of track linking Matlock Riverside with Rowsley South.

(Above) : As the road sign indicates, No D9016 'Gordon Highlander' is seen on a low loader approaching Darley Dale on 12 May bound for Peak Rail.

(Below) : I must confess being unable to resist including this image if, for no other reason, than the colours displayed on a poor-looking D6831 (No 37131) waiting at Rowsley South on 2nd March for a move to the Harry Needle Railway Company at Barrow Hill for repair.

(Above) : One of the original ten Class 44 'Peak' locomotives, No D8 'Penyghent', adorned in the smart Brunswick green livery with half-yellow front end and red sole bar departs Darley Dale Station on 22nd September.

(Below) : Meanwhile, No 31421 'Wigan Pier' (31270) freshly repainted in Regional Railways livery is seen approaching Darley Dale on the same day.   (All Paul Biggs)

AKNOWLEDGEMENTS

Many thanks go to all the people who have kindly contributed images for inclusion in this title who are named below, along with an access reference for of any personal photographic website, should you wish to see more of their photographic exploits:

ALLEN, Anthony	Salisbury	
BALL, Ian	Thirsk	northeastheavy.fototopic.net
BALLANTYNE, Hugh	Eccleshall	
BIGGS, Paul	Loughborough	paulbiggs.fototopic.net
BINCH, John	Harborne	
BLOIS, Martin	High Wycombe	
BUCKLEY, Justin	Erdington	ticketmans.fototopic.net
CAMERON, Donald	Milngavie	
EDGE, Ralf	Derby	ralfedge.co.uk
ELY, Marc	Brighton	
GATEHOUSE, Don	Bromsgrove	
GIBBS, Nigel	Bedford	
GILES, Richard	Clevedon	
GORSE, Carl	Hartlepool	37682.fototopic.net
HARKNESS, Martin	Oswaldwistle	
HAZELDEN, Alan	Tunbridge Wells	
KAY, Anthony	Romford	anthonykay.fototopic.net
JONES, Richard	Chislehurst	railphotos.demeseo.com
JOYNSON, Nic	Ringwood	
KERR, Fred	Southport	
MAKEPEACE, Jonathan	Surbiton	
McGOVERN, Keith	Mussleburgh	
MORRISON, Brian	Sidcup	
NAYLOR, Andrew	Carnforth	andrewstransport.fototopic.net
PLUMB, Geoff	Aylesbury	geoff-plumb.fototopic.net
RAMSAY, Jim	Carnoustie	tayrail.fototopic.net
RUDD, John	Peterborough	
SHERMAN, Karl	Sunderland	rail-images.co.uk
SHERWOOD, Robert	Paignton	southwestrailways.fototopic.net
SLOCOMBE, Nick	London	trainsofthewesternworld.fototopic.net
SMALL, Andy	Leicester	andy4585.fototopic.net
STRACEY, David	Chinnor	
TANDY, Peter	Stratford on Avon	petertandy.co.uk
TERRACE, Robert	Hatfield	robterrace.co.uk
TINDALL, Mick	Sutton in Ashfield	mpt-trains.fototopic.net
WELHAM, James	Great Leighs	jameswelham.fototopic.net